# THE REAL BAPTISM
# OF THE HOLY SPIRIT

## When it occurs and what it involves

# THE REAL
# BAPTISM
## of the Holy Spirit

When it occurs and what it involves

# Peter Masters

THE WAKEMAN TRUST, LONDON

**THE REAL BAPTISM OF THE HOLY SPIRIT**

© Peter Masters

First published under the title *Only One Baptism of the Holy Spirit,* 1994
This edition 2018

THE WAKEMAN TRUST
(Wakeman Trust is a UK Registered Charity)

Wakeman Trust UK Registered Office
38 Walcot Square
London SE11 4TZ

Wakeman Trust USA Office
300 Artino Drive
Oberlin, OH 44074-1263

Website: www.wakemantrust.org

ISBN 978 1 908919 91 5

Cover design by Andrew Owen

Printed by Stephens & George, Merthyr Tydfil, UK

# Contents

1   When is a Believer Baptised With the Spirit?         7

2   Is a Second Baptism Needed for Assurance?           21

3   How Does the Spirit Witness With Our Spirit?        25

4   The Spirit of Holiness                              37

5   Attending the Wrong Classroom                       43

6   Are We to Fight Sin?                                49

7   Must We Be Emptied or Broken?                       53

8   The Filling of the Spirit                           57

9   The Spirit's Way                                    65

10  A Baptism of Bliss?                                 75

11  The Case of the Ephesus Twelve                      79

# 1

# When is a Believer
# Baptised With the Spirit?

THE VIEW THAT EVERYONE who is converted to Christ needs a further baptism of the Spirit, or a 'second blessing', used to be a fringe teaching among Bible-believing Christians. In the last 50 years, however, it has become a main plank of the charismatic movement worldwide, and has even penetrated the ranks of conservative churches. Most charismatic writers refer with disdain to 'traditional' believers, whom they see as third-rate Christians who obstinately refuse to receive the fulness of the Spirit. Some speak of 'hidebound traditionalists'.

But where do charismatic teachers and those who share their views about the baptism of the Spirit get their ideas from? The answer, most of the time, is from teachers who approach the Bible in a surprisingly careless manner, virtually ignoring the Bible's own rules of interpretation. Those who promote a baptism of the

Spirit after conversion tend to pluck texts out of context, paying no attention to the fact that other Bible passages *on the same subject* contradict their interpretations.

This was the complaint of a famous Bible teacher named William Biederwolf, who in 1913 protested about the many contradictory statements on the Holy Spirit which were made by some preachers in his day. He noticed that these statements, though dogmatic, were seldom supported by texts, and when they were, a mere glance at the text showed that it did not confirm the preachers' claims. Dr Biederwolf set himself the task of assembling all the Scripture references to different aspects of the work of the Spirit, and produced a book that stands today as a classic.*

The idea that Christians need a baptism of the Spirit after and in addition to their conversion is simply not borne out by the Bible. This chapter will take a look at all the texts which tell us *when* the believer is baptised with the Spirit. We guarantee that after reviewing this group of texts with an open mind, the reader will never again accept the claims about the baptism of the Spirit which are presented in the books of charismatic (and 'higher-life' or 'deeper-life' or so-called 'continuist') authors.

Before reviewing the texts, let me say a word about the importance of this issue. The idea that there is a baptism of the Spirit after conversion has sent numerous Christians into a cloudland of unreal emotional experiences, imagined revelations, and even delusions of perfect holiness. Many others have been plunged into heartache and confusion because they could not get the 'baptism' they sought. Yet every day, in charismatic gatherings large and small, people are being persuaded to seek this blessing. In a fevered environment, urged on by the prayers and appeals of others, they receive the laying-on of hands, and are taught how to utter sounds that will 'trigger' their speaking in a tongue.

---

* *A Help to the Study of the Holy Spirit*, W. E. Biederwolf, Wakeman Trust, London

Some become so anxious to obtain the 'baptism' that their priorities change entirely. Instead of their priority being to please and serve the Lord by their witness and increasing holiness, their supreme objective has become that of getting a dramatic sensation of the Spirit in their life. They hear and read the claims of the 'Spirit-filled' people, and all their supposed spiritual accomplishments, and become convinced that authentic Christianity is a matter of ecstatic feelings, personal revelations and special power.

In today's environment of spiritual confusion, it is essential to realise that the only baptism of the Spirit mentioned in the Bible is the gracious act of the Spirit when he comes to dwell within the believer at the time of conversion. Once he is within the soul, the true believer has him, and possesses him entirely. Of course, we shall want an increasing experience of his strengthening and illumination, but we should never look for an extra, additional baptism, craving ecstatic, curious, mystical experiences, as though a large part of the Spirit was left out when he entered into our lives at conversion. These statements we shall prove from the texts.

Our task, once we are converted, is to begin immediately to co-operate with the Spirit, to walk by his power, and to prove his helpfulness more and more. It is as we walk in the Spirit that we will taste and know more of his power and blessing.

In the light of the claims which are being made in support of a further baptism with the Spirit *after* conversion, can it be proved that conversion includes the entire entry of the Spirit into the life of the believer? Is this a matter which is open to debate because the Scriptures are unclear? The fact is that the Bible is unmistakably clear on this subject. We are provided with a large array of texts which prove utterly and repeatedly that the Holy Spirit comes personally to dwell within every child of God at conversion, and not in stages. Here are the 'proof texts' which establish the traditional reformed teaching beyond all doubt. In this chapter they are presented for convenience in order of their appearance in the Bible.

## Proof text no. 1 – *Acts 2.38*

The first is in *Acts 2.38*, where Peter says – 'Repent, and be baptised every one of you in the name of Jesus Christ for the remission of sins, and ye shall receive the gift of the Holy Ghost.'

In this text it is made clear that the giving of the gift of the Holy Spirit is totally bound up with the experience of repenting and coming to Christ. The unqualified promise of God is that the Holy Spirit will definitely come to people when they are converted.

This would seem to be an unanswerable proof text, but those who want to separate between the Holy Spirit's work at conversion and a subsequent baptism, say that Peter is not referring to *baptism* with the Holy Spirit, but merely to an *initial gift* of the Spirit. They agree that the Holy Spirit is involved at conversion, but they say that this is something which the Spirit does by himself, whereas Christ promised that he would personally baptise his people with the Holy Spirit.

By making this strange distinction, they ingeniously produce two baptisms out of one. So, according to these teachers, there remains another blessing to be experienced after conversion. (Dr Martyn Lloyd-Jones, though not altogether charismatic, taught this idea in the last years of his ministry.)

However, Peter disqualifies this novel doubling-up approach by telling us that the gift of the Spirit which he speaks of is the very same baptism which the Lord Jesus promised to give. He says – 'This Jesus hath God raised up, whereof we all are witnesses. Therefore being by the right hand of God exalted, and having received of the Father the promise of the Holy Ghost, he hath shed forth this, which ye now see and hear' *(Acts 2.32-33)*. In other words, the gift of the Spirit poured out on the Day of Pentecost (and promised subsequently to every believer at conversion) was nothing other than the gift of the Holy Spirit as promised by Christ. There can therefore be no further baptism after this.

Peter says that this baptism will come to 'every one' who repents, and this will continue to happen throughout the ongoing history of the church, 'for the promise is unto you, and to your children, and to all that are afar off, even as many as the Lord our God shall call' *(Acts 2.39).* Wherever the Gospel is preached, among all nations, and for all subsequent generations, the gift of the Holy Spirit will come to sinners at the time they repent and are saved.

Some say that this makes the baptism of the Spirit a secret, silent, passionless affair, but this is not the case. True conversion is accompanied by joy in the Holy Spirit and much assurance. The new convert longs to see other souls saved, and begins the Christian life with wonder and gratitude, light and love, zeal and fervour. Strong feeling marks the true baptism of the Spirit experienced as part of conversion.

What was the result of the Holy Spirit's coming to those who were converted on the Day of Pentecost? Did they speak in tongues? Did they work healing miracles? As far as the vast majority of converts were concerned, the record of *Acts* does not say they did. When people become influenced by charismatic teaching they frequently assume that the gifts of tongues, prophecy and healing were distributed among all the 3,000 converts on the Day of Pentecost, but although there is a very detailed description of the new lifestyle and pattern of behaviour of these converts in *Acts 2.41-47,* there is not one reference to these converts manifesting such gifts. The idea that commonly prevails among charismatic believers is simply not in line with the data in the New Testament. At the most, only the 120 original disciples are said to have spoken in foreign languages which they had never learned. There is no mention of the 3,000 doing so, nor the vast number who were converted soon afterwards. *Acts* says that only the members of the apostolic band (including three close helpers) worked healing miracles.

The converts at the time of Pentecost received the Spirit personally and individually as they were converted, and the result was that they – 'continued stedfastly in the apostles' doctrine', and so on. They became devoted to the Word of God, gained a deep spiritual bond with other converts, discovered how to really pray and worship, and were filled with awe and wonder – all because the work and baptism of the Spirit had made things so real to them. As we have pointed out, these effects are all listed in *Acts 2.42-47*, along with a description of their unity of heart, their sacrificial sharing of goods, and their great fervour and sincerity of heart. *These* were the results of the Spirit entering their lives at conversion.

Of course, there was also a public dimension to the outpouring of the Spirit upon the new Christian church on the Day of Pentecost, for it was the inauguration day of the church of Jesus Christ, when the Spirit of God signalled to the world (and especially to the Jews) that the church was now the Temple of God, and the pillar and ground of the Truth.

## Proof text no. 2 – *Romans 5.1-5*

Our second text to prove that the baptism of the Spirit takes place only at conversion is *Romans 5.1-5*. In this vital passage Paul writes – 'Therefore being justified by faith, we have peace with God through our Lord Jesus Christ: by whom also we have access by faith into this grace wherein we stand, and rejoice in hope of the glory of God. And...the love of God is shed abroad in our hearts by the Holy Ghost which is given unto us.'

When is the Holy Spirit given to us? Paul answers – at the time of our justification (conversion). The wonderful, deeply feelingful experience of having the love of God shed abroad in our hearts is rooted back in our conversion. Newer translations usually make the passage even clearer by bringing out the *tense* of Paul's statement in the original Greek: 'The love of God has been poured out within our hearts through the Holy Spirit who was given to us.'

Some teachers drive a great wedge between the experience of conversion described in *Romans 5.1*, and the deep experience of love described in *Romans 5.5*, saying that the love of God is shed abroad in our hearts when we get a subsequent baptism of the Spirit. But the whole point of Paul's statement is to say that the receiving of the Spirit is the comfort and privilege of everyone without exception who has been born again.

## Proof text no. 3 – *Romans 8.9* and *15*

*Romans 8.9* and *8.15* are also verses which prove that the baptism of the Spirit occurs at conversion. In verse 9 Paul says: 'But ye are not in the flesh, but in the Spirit, if so be that the Spirit of God dwell in you. Now if any man have not the Spirit of Christ, he is none of his.' In verse 15 he says – 'For ye have not received the spirit of bondage again to fear; but ye have received the Spirit of adoption, whereby we cry, Abba, Father.'

We note that Paul gives the Holy Spirit a name – *the Spirit of adoption*. Conversion involves our being adopted into the family of God. It is the Holy Spirit who brings this about and who teaches us to say, 'Abba, Father,' the intimate, familiar cry of every child of God. Nothing could be more artificial and forced than to split this passage into two parts, claiming that the second part suddenly begins to speak of a special and rarefied experience received only through a subsequent second blessing of the Spirit. This interpretation adds to the text words that are not there. The plain and natural sense of the passage is:

(a) Every Christian, however young in the faith, has the Holy Spirit dwelling within. (In other words, the Spirit enters at conversion.)

(b) The 'Abba, Father' instinct enters our hearts with the indwelling Spirit from the very moment of *adoption* or conversion, and not at some later stage.

## Proof text no. 4 – *1 Corinthians 6.11, 19-20*

*1 Corinthians 6* includes verses which demonstrate that the gift of the Spirit is part of our conversion. Paul says (v 11) – 'Ye are washed ... sanctified ... justified in the name of the Lord Jesus, and by the Spirit of our God.' Then he says (vv 19-20) – 'Know ye not that your body is the temple of the Holy Ghost which is in you, which ye have of God, and ye are not your own? For ye are bought with a price.'

In these verses Paul includes *all* believers at Corinth, reminding them that they have experienced all the components of conversion by the Spirit, that they have him, and that he indwells them. The Spirit, he shows, indwells from the time believers are 'bought with a price', which means from the day of their conversion.

## Proof text no. 5 – *1 Corinthians 12.13*

*1 Corinthians 12.13* demonstrates very clearly that the baptism of the Spirit occurs at conversion.* 'For by one Spirit are we all baptised into one body, whether we be Jews or Gentiles, whether we be bond or free; and have been all made to drink into one Spirit.' Every believer has been baptised into (which means *placed into*) the body of Christ by the Holy Spirit. Obviously, it is at conversion that we enter the family or body of Christ. As a result, all have been made to drink of the same Holy Spirit, which means that the Holy Spirit is within each one.

Some teachers protest that because this is a baptism carried out by the Spirit himself, it cannot be the same as the baptism *with* the Spirit which Christ promised to give to believers. However, being 'made to drink into one Spirit' is without doubt the same thing as being baptised with the Spirit by Christ. We may be certain of this because Paul uses here the very word for the baptism of the Spirit which Christ himself used in *John 7.37-39*. Note how the Lord used the word *drink* as a description of the receiving of the Spirit:–

---

* Baptism by the Spirit is mentioned only seven times in the entire New Testament. Four of these references are in the Gospels, and all record John the Baptist saying that Christ would baptise with the Spirit. One text is the promise of Christ to baptise with the Spirit *(Acts 1.5)*. Another text is *Acts 11.16*, which is about the 'mini-Pentecost' in the house of Cornelius.

'In the last day, that great day of the feast, Jesus stood and cried, saying, If any man thirst, let him come unto me, and drink. He that believeth on me, as the scripture hath said, out of his belly shall flow rivers of living water. (But this spake he of the Spirit, which they that believe on him should receive: for the Holy Ghost was not yet given; because that Jesus was not yet glorified.)'

When we come to Christ for salvation and drink of him, we automatically drink of the Holy Spirit as well, and he dwells within us (with dramatic results) from that moment. *1 Corinthians 12.13*, therefore, proves that all believers, at conversion, are placed into the body of Christ by the Spirit, and simultaneously baptised with the Holy Spirit.

In view of the fact that Paul refers to Spirit-baptism only once in all his epistles, and then strictly in connection with conversion, how can charismatic teachers hijack the term to describe a second, subsequent experience of the Spirit? 'Traditional' evangelical teaching calls all subsequent pronounced blessings by the Spirit by terms such as fillings and strengthenings, not baptisms.

## Proof text no. 6 – *Galatians 3.2*

*Galatians 3.2* proves beyond all argument that the Holy Spirit is poured out by Christ at the time that sinners come to saving faith. The Galatians were being drawn away by Judaisers into the error of justification by works. In this context Paul exclaims – 'This only would I learn of you, Received ye the Spirit by the works of the law, or by the hearing of faith?' *(Galatians 3.2.)* Clearly, he is saying that the Holy Spirit is imparted to believers when they hear the Truth and believe.

A few verses later *(Galatians 3.13-14)* Paul reminds his readers that the promise of the Holy Spirit is received through faith in the redeeming work of Christ. Once again, therefore, the receiving of Christ's promise of the Spirit is linked with the moment of *saving* faith.

## Proof text no. 7 – *Galatians 4.4-6*

In *Galatians 4.4-6* the link between conversion and the receiving of the Holy Spirit is emphasised yet again as Paul says – 'But when the fulness of the time was come, God sent forth his Son, made of a woman, made under the law, to redeem them that were under the law, that we might receive the adoption of sons. And because ye are sons, God hath sent forth the Spirit of his Son into your hearts, crying, Abba, Father.'

It could not be more clearly expressed that at the time that we receive adoption as children, God sends the Spirit into our hearts, enabling us to cry, 'Abba, Father.' 'Wherefore,' Paul goes on to say in the very next verse, 'thou art no more a servant, but a son.' This sending of the Spirit into the heart can be nothing other than the baptism of the Spirit, therefore every true believer without exception receives this blessing at the time of conversion. In texts like this there is no basis for the idea that conversion is separated from the imparting of the Spirit.

## Proof text no. 8 – *Ephesians 1.3*

In *Ephesians 1.3* neither the giving nor the indwelling of the Holy Spirit are mentioned, but the verse nevertheless completely eliminates the idea that Christian believers may be divided into 'haves' and 'have-nots' on the matter of whether they have been baptised with the Spirit. *All* the 'saints' at Ephesus are said by Paul to have been blessed 'with all spiritual blessings in heavenly places in Christ'. Paul insists here that every believer is given *every* spiritual blessing by virtue of being in Christ. As Dr William Hendriksen wrote, 'The very word *every* clearly proves that it would be wrong to subtract even a single invisible bounty from the list of those "vast benefits divine which we in Christ possess", yet the context indicates that the apostle is thinking particularly of those that are mentioned in the present paragraph, namely *election . . . redemption . . .* and *certification* (sealing) as sons and heirs.'

The apostle will go on to say that *every* spiritual blessing includes the sealing of the Spirit, given to all who are 'in Christ'. We must reject any interpretation which separates either the sealing or baptism of the Spirit from conversion and makes it the possession of only *some* believers. The idea is completely out of line with all the grand, authoritative apostolic statements.

## Proof text no. 9 – *Ephesians 1.13-14*

*Ephesians 1.13-14,* referred to above, provides yet another solid proof text for the doctrine that the baptism of the Holy Spirit *always* occurs at conversion. These verses read: 'In whom ye also trusted, after that ye heard the word of truth, the gospel of your salvation: in whom also after that ye believed, ye were sealed with that holy Spirit of promise, which is the earnest of our inheritance until the redemption of the purchased possession, unto the praise of his glory.'

The sense of the Greek original is 'When you heard . . . and believed in him, you were sealed,' showing that being sealed with the Holy Spirit is the inevitable consequence of believing. It is part of conversion.

The sealing of the Spirit refers to the receiving of authenticating signs, by which the new convert (and those who look on) may be certain that the Spirit has given him new life, and placed him on the road to Heaven. The idea of sealing also includes security. This sealing is clearly an aspect of the baptism and indwelling of the Spirit, for the new believer is sealed with the Spirit. This occurs, the passage informs us, as a pledge or 'deposit' to assure us that our salvation will be carried through to Heaven by the Lord. The plain meaning of the passage is that God gives this wonderful guarantee to *every* recipient of grace. He does not merely give it to some, or even to many, but to all.

Everyone understands the value of a guarantee. What trader gives a guarantee to *some* customers while withholding it from others? If people buy new homes or new appliances, they expect the guarantee to be certain. They would be unable to believe their ears if the salesman said, 'A guarantee? Oh, you may get one; on the other hand you may not. You will have to see as time goes on whether you are one of the fortunate ones who is given a guarantee.'

When God gives a pledge and a guarantee to his people, he gives it to them all. Accordingly, when we believe, the Holy Spirit enters in, and his first gracious work is to give us a foretaste of our future blessings; a 'placental' experience of spiritual benefits.

## Proof text no. 10 – *Ephesians 4.30*

*Ephesians 4.30* also confirms that all believers are sealed by the Holy Spirit, and not merely some. Modern translations correctly employ the past tense in this verse: 'And do not grieve the Holy Spirit of God, by whom you *were* sealed for the day of redemption' (1977 *NASB*). Paul does not say that some of them were sealed, or even most of them, but he is certain that all who are truly converted were sealed when they were brought into the Christian life.

## Proof text no. 11 – *1 Thessalonians 1.5-6*

*1 Thessalonians 1.5-6* firmly places the Spirit's baptism of joy right alongside the experience of conversion, Paul saying – 'For our gospel came not unto you in word only, but also in power, and in the Holy Ghost, and in much assurance; as ye know what manner of men we were among you for your sake. And ye became followers of us, and of the Lord, having received the word in much affliction, with joy of the Holy Ghost.' The apostle presents this overwhelming experience of the Spirit as having been part of conversion for all the converts of Thessalonica. The people savingly grasped and received the Word, receiving as they did so the joy of the Holy Spirit.

## Proof text no. 12 – *1 John 4.12-13*

*1 John 4.12-13* is one of two similar proof texts in the same epistle. It reads: 'If we love one another, God dwelleth in us, and his love is perfected in us. Hereby know we that we dwell in him, and he in us, because he hath given us of his Spirit.' Also, at the end of the previous chapter, John says – 'And hereby we know that he abideth in us, by the Spirit which he hath given us.'

In these words the apostle John makes no allowance for the possibility that some truly converted Christians may not yet have received the baptism of (or with) the Spirit. In John's 'tests of life', the baptism and indwelling of the Holy Spirit are inseparable from the presence of spiritual life itself.

## The traditional view

The natural sense of all these passages is that the baptism of the Holy Spirit (and his sealing) occurs as part of the conversion of the believer. By contrast, passages which are claimed in support of a separate, post-conversion baptism of the Spirit are never plain and straightforward. Complex exegetical gymnastics have to be accomplished in order to make any semblance of a case for this second blessing.

The texts we have just examined confirm the historic position of mainstream evangelicalism on the baptism of the Spirit. This is the viewpoint so perfectly summarised in the *Baptist Confession of Faith of 1689* in the following words: 'All those that are justified . . . receive the Spirit of adoption . . . are enabled to cry "Abba, Father," are pitied, protected, provided for, and chastened by him, as by a Father; yet never cast off; but sealed to the day of redemption . . .' (chapter 12).

## What about the Ephesus twelve?

When charismatic and other second-blessing writers present their case for a baptism of the Spirit in addition to conversion, they nearly always point to what happened at Ephesus when Paul discovered a group of Jewish believers there, former disciples of John the Baptist. The reasoning goes along these lines: Paul found a company of about twelve men who believed that Christ was the Messiah. On discovering that they were ignorant of the Holy Spirit, he laid hands upon them and they received the Spirit and spoke in tongues. All this proves that the baptism of the Spirit is to be received as a separate blessing, after conversion, and that it may (most charismatics say *will*) be accompanied by speaking in tongues.

Is this a sound and reasonable interpretation of the events at Ephesus? The resounding answer of the vast majority of evangelical Bible commentators through church history is that it is not. The traditional evangelical explanation of what took place at Ephesus is set out in chapter 11 at the end of this book, together with the reasons why it is wrong to read into the passage a second baptism of the Spirit. Readers are invited to read this chapter – *The Case of the Ephesus Twelve.*

# 2
# Is a Second Baptism
# Needed for Assurance?

**M**OST OF THOSE who teach the need for a baptism of the Spirit after conversion, claim that this is essential for sanctification. This is the prevailing viewpoint among charismatics, and all 'higher-life' teachers. They say that once a Christian receives this subsequent baptism, all the effort of living a holy life is taken over by the indwelling Holy Spirit, giving success and victory to the believer.

Some teachers, however, especially in recent years, have advanced a different benefit as the chief value of this additional baptism of the Holy Spirit. Their idea is that such a baptism is the only source of truly satisfying joy and assurance. The need of a second blessing or baptism for assurance is argued from the words of Paul in *Romans 8.15*: 'For ye have not received the spirit of bondage again to fear;

but ye have received the Spirit of adoption, whereby we cry, Abba, Father.' The expression 'Abba, Father' is seized upon and turned into an exalted cry of ecstatic certainty and assurance. 'This,' say these teachers, 'is nothing other than the most intimate form of assurance causing a glorious sense of sonship to well up within the believer, overwhelming the soul. At such a moment this believer will have no doubt whatsoever that he is a child of God, being filled with sublime joy. This is the direct infusion of great assurance which is clearly not the general experience of most Christians today. It is nothing less than a baptism with the Holy Spirit!'

The first comment to be made on this interpretation of *Romans 8.15* is that the context warns against it. We must remember that Paul has just said (in verse 9) that the Spirit of God already dwells in every true Christian, without exception. We must also note (as seen in chapter 1 of this book) that Paul says that the 'Spirit of adoption' causes us to say, 'Abba, Father,' which makes this loving cry begin from the time of our adoption (conversion). Also, we should be aware that the advocates of a special baptism greatly inflate the meaning of the words 'Abba, Father,' in making them speak of a rarefied and heavenly sensation of assurance. Some writers get completely carried away at this point, developing a wildly fanciful idea of the meaning of the term.

Paul's words are meant to be a comfort to all ordinary Christians, describing the deep sense of love, belonging and closeness that every true believer may experience at the throne of grace from the day of conversion. They were never intended to teach the availability of an *extraordinary* and mystical level of assurance resulting from a special baptism, and they should not be snatched away from ordinary believers in order to nourish the quest for ecstatic experience.

In *Romans 8.15-16*, Paul effectively tells us that one of the glorious benefits of true conversion is that even though we may go through periods of failure and trial, we always have admission into the presence of our Father, for we know how to pray. We know the way 'home'. We can always find our way to the place of mercy and help, assured that we are accepted in Christ, and there we may pour out our hearts before him. Paul simply says that because we are adopted children we instinctively know how to cry out to our Father, and we may have intimate access into his presence at any time.

If we are truly converted, we do not have the superstitious, frightened attitude of pagans, who desperately offer sacrifices in a vain hope that their gods will hear them. Nor do we, like the formal worshippers among the Jews, hope against hope that priests, sacrifices and other ceremonies will secure the favour of an otherwise unknowable God. Whether we are deeply or moderately assured in our feelings, we may be certain that God will forgive us and receive us because he is *our Father*, and we are adopted children. This is what Paul is saying, and it gives comfort and encouragement to us all, and not only to supposedly 'super-spiritual' people.

A small child may be resentful towards his parents because of some punishment he has received, or because he wants something which has been withheld from him. Or he may be completely preoccupied in play, so that he is not, for the time being, interested in his parents. But he never loses his awareness that he is his parents' child, or that he belongs in the house. He is never afraid to run to his parents if he needs something. He never forgets the way from the garden into the house, or what his parents look like. Paul's great cry of 'Abba, Father' simply means that we know that God is our own Father, and that we can always count on his care. 'Abba' was the personal and familiar Aramaic word for father, and it is used by Paul to emphasise the personal bond between believers and their heavenly Father. Sad and troubled people would use this simple and beautiful word in addressing their father, just as elated, happy people would. The Lord Jesus Christ used it in the Garden of Gethsemane when his soul was 'exceeding sorrowful unto death'. He prayed that the hour might pass from him. 'Sore amazed, and ... very heavy', he prayed, 'Abba, Father.' If the Saviour could use this term in his greatest hour of anguish, it is obviously wrong to insist that it always and only signifies elevated, ecstatic, joyous feelings.

Even the word *cry* is pressed into service by Spirit-baptism teachers in support of the idea that 'Abba Father' refers to a sublime higher level of feeling flowing from a special baptism of the Spirit. They claim that the intensity of the Greek verb confirms the depth of assurance being experienced by the person who addresses the Father with these words. However, the very same verb is used in the Bible in connection with cries of anguish, dismay, need, and even hatred and opposition. It is used of the final cry of the Saviour *(Matthew 27.50)* in the hour of his forsakenness, when he yielded up the spirit. It is certainly a very feelingful cry, but it can be the cry of a suffering person, or a downhearted, needy, despondent soul, just as much as that of a rejoicing person.

Without doubt, the plain sense of this 'Abba, Father' passage is to teach that all genuine children know how to approach their heavenly Father, and can fall before him in true repentance and with heartfelt love at any time. To find in this term evidence for a higher, mystical experience involves fanciful, forced and false exegesis of the passage. There is a wonderful form of assurance which comes to us from the ordinary work of the Spirit in our lives, and this we shall examine in the next chapter.

# 3
## How Does the Spirit Witness With Our Spirit?

P AUL HAS BEEN SPEAKING in *Romans 8.15* of how the Holy Spirit imparts to believers a personal consciousness that God is now their Father, the doctrine of assurance. Then, in verse 16, he turns to the way in which the Spirit bears witness to their salvation in a more direct way. He says: 'The Spirit itself beareth witness with our spirit, that we are the children of God.' The question is, how does the Holy Spirit witness with our spirit?

First, we must be clear on what Paul does not mean here. He does not say that the Holy Spirit is poured out in a special baptism, thereby flooding the soul with *direct* divine assurance. While our sovereign, gracious God may at times grant very remarkable seasons of special assurance to his people, this is not what is in mind in this verse, for Paul is presenting what should be the normal, everyday experience of Christians in the life of prayer.

Some writers describe only two forms of assurance: first, that which is deduced from the Bible, and secondly, an elevated form which comes directly from the Spirit of God. They regard the first as a rather pedestrian form of assurance, because believers must glean it for themselves. They must read the Bible and find passages which describe the signs or tests of true conversion (eg: *Acts 2.42 ff*; *1 John*). Then, as they read, they will be able to say, 'This has certainly happened to me, therefore I must be truly saved.'

But then, they tell us, we must move on to the higher, superior type of assurance – an overwhelming sense of wonder and sonship which comes directly from the Spirit as the result of a special baptism. In reality, the gift of direct and intense assurance is more occasional. It would appear to be a special kindness given to believers in times of great oppression or grief or exertion. It cannot be worked up, for it is a sovereign prerogative of the Spirit.

It is wrong to teach that an elevated sense of God is the normal experience of the believer, because to do so gives great alarm to all who do not find this to be their everyday experience, throwing many earnest souls into seeking an imaginary Spirit-baptism. More seriously, this teaching leaps over the most common form of assurance, not even recognising its existence. Lying between the assurance which may be deduced from the Bible, and the occasional kind which the Spirit gives in a direct way, there is a rich and rewarding form of regular, daily assurance available to all believers. This is the form spoken of by the apostle Paul in *Romans 8.16*. It is the constant interaction of the Holy Spirit in our lives as we pray to God for help in dealing with our sins, and also for help with all the other needs and problems faced every day, especially in our witness and service for the Lord.

It is an immense and constant source of assurance to have a continuous flow of answers to our prayers, including prayers for guidance and help in understanding the Word. All are abundantly answered. It is so sad that some teachers, in their preoccupation with the idea of a special baptism, entirely overlook the everyday supply of assurance which springs from experimental Christian living, or day-to-day praying and proving. It is clear from all that Paul has been saying in the preceding verses that this is the true meaning of the Spirit witnessing with our spirit. He has just said: 'Therefore, brethren, we are debtors, not to the flesh, to live after the flesh. For if ye live after the flesh, ye shall die: but if ye through the Spirit do mortify the deeds of the body, ye shall live. For as many as are led by the Spirit of God, they are the sons of God' *(Romans 8.12-14)*.

The subject here is putting to death the deeds of the flesh by the help of the Spirit. Those who prayerfully engage in the fight against personal sin find to their joy that they are actively helped by the Spirit, and this is a massive and uplifting source of encouragement, as we shall see in chapter six – *Are We to Fight Sin?* Paul gives us a picture of Christians whose consciences are (as the result of prayer) made lively by the Spirit, and who therefore become concerned about sin. They long to make progress, keeping a watch on their behaviour and praying for help in putting to death wrong thoughts, desires and actions. By so walking in daily co-operation with the Spirit, they experience *through the help they receive* the sure 'witness' of the Spirit that they are children of God.

This form of assurance is truly authenticating, because it rests on evidence, something real being achieved, namely, better conduct and character. Only genuinely regenerate people hunger and thirst after righteousness, hate their sin, and long to please and serve the Lord in obedience to his commandments. Only genuine converts experience victory over sin. This is truly authenticating and gives rise to tremendous gratitude, joy and assurance.

Supremely, the Holy Spirit confirms that he is our Guardian by his unmistakable help in answer to prayer. Time after time we are given grace to overcome some trial, and strengthened to stand up to great difficulties. Repeatedly we are given cause to thank and praise God for hearing and answering our prayers, and so the Spirit adds his testimony to our realisation that we are the children of God.

If, therefore, we lack assurance, it may be that our flow of 'evidence' (through answered prayer) has dried up. Have we stopped praying? Do we no longer seek specific help about particular problems or sins? Have we stopped striving for holiness? Have we ceased noticing the answers to our prayers? Why do we crave after *direct* assurance, as though we had no evidence from answered prayer? Are we not engaged in any hard Christian service, which leads us to earnest prayer, and therefore to the very many answers which will inevitably follow?

Let us leave the provision of *direct* feelings of assurance to the Lord. If our God chooses to pour upon us at some time an extra level of awareness that we are his children, and an unusually enlightened sense of his love for us, then that is his sovereign prerogative. It is not the everyday expectation of the believer. If it were, then this would not be a life of faith. Let us not demand the elevated experiences as if they were our daily right.

Let us rejoice in the fact that our faith may be wonderfully strengthened as we read the signs of conversion in the Word. But let it be strengthened even more as we notice and give thanks for the vast number of clear answers to our prayers.

The *help* of the Spirit is one of the great themes of *Romans 8*. If we do not strive for personal advance in sanctification, or if we have no avenue of Christian service, and bear no burdens in the Lord's work, then we will have no burning needs, and few truly significant things to pray for. Consequently we will suffer a tragic lack of evidence of the Spirit's help, and therefore have little assurance. Those who are 'hearers only' miss most of the real blessing.

It is sometimes believers lacking assurance for these reasons who begin to crave a more direct form of assurance. Be warned: this is the high road to mysticism and self-delusion. Some believers want a blessing, but not on the Lord's terms. They want assurance without Christian service or commitment. But the Lord has determined that most assurance will come through the evidences of the Spirit's help in daily sanctification, witness and service.

So important is this matter that it must be proved by reference to other passages of Scripture. Where else, then, does Scripture spell out the fact that much of our assurance must come from experiencing the interaction and help of the Spirit in answer to our prayers, especially prayers for help in sanctification and service?

The following paragraphs provide a rapid review of key passages, showing that throughout the New Testament the apostolic teaching never varies on this point. Assurance is constantly described as flowing from the struggle against sin, and from the practice of praying to God for help in all the affairs of life. Believers are meant to build up a great memory-bank of all God's goodness and power towards them, and thus become increasingly *convinced*. Look, for example, at the prayer of Paul for the Christians at Ephesus, which begins in *Ephesians 1.17*, proceeds into a glorious doctrinal affirmation, and resumes as a prayer from *Ephesians 3.14*.

Paul first prays that the Holy Spirit will illuminate the Ephesian believers (already sealed with the Spirit at their conversion according to *Ephesians 1.13*) so that they may fully grasp the wonder of their future inheritance, and the power of God in saving, keeping, protecting and sanctifying them on the way to glory. Two great sources of assurance are referred to in the opening part of the prayer – the Word, and the power of God.

Then, in *Ephesians 3.14-16*, Paul prays: 'For this cause I bow my knees unto the Father of our Lord Jesus Christ, of whom the whole family in heaven and earth is named, that he would grant you, according to the riches of his glory, to be strengthened with might by his Spirit in the inner man.'

Note once again that these Ephesians were already *sealed* with the Spirit at conversion, yet they still needed to be 'strengthened with might by his Spirit in the inner man'. Even though the Spirit is within us from conversion we constantly need strengthening because the Holy Spirit does not give us all the strength we require for our entire

Christian life in one bestowal. The strengthening of the Spirit is something continuous, and even conditional, for we must pray for help, and keep the terms and conditions for blessing.

For what do we need all this strengthening? The language of Paul reminds us that while here we are in a battle for holiness and service for the Lord. Paul is not praying for indolent Christians who want assurance without attempting to serve the Lord or struggle against sin, but for those who will pursue holiness and commit themselves to spreading the Gospel, speaking for the Saviour, and serving side by side with fellow-labourers in the church. He is praying for those who will strive against the allurements of this world. It is such Christians for whom Paul prays, 'that Christ may dwell in your hearts by faith; that ye, being rooted and grounded in love, may be able to comprehend . . . the breadth, and length, and depth, and height; and to know the love of Christ, which passeth knowledge . . .' *(Ephesians 3.17-19).* Take first the words – '*rooted and grounded* in love'. As we pray for help in holiness and service, we receive strength to be stable, patient and disciplined in our love for the Lord, and we then derive much assurance from the fact that the Spirit enables such weak, unstable people as we are to stand firm. We find we are not uprooted and hurled aside like poorly-rooted trees in a storm, but that we stand firm against all the temptations of the devil, the temptations of the world, and the inclination to laziness or cowardice in witness.

Paul then prays that such believers may grasp 'the breadth, and length, and depth, and height' and know 'the love of Christ, which passeth knowledge'. We desire the assurance which shines out from these words, but let us never forget that the route to this assurance passes first through the battlefield where sin is fought, and also through the servants' hall.

The 'formula' for assurance and blessedness is the same throughout the New Testament. How do we obtain assurance? First things first: we must want to please the Lord in the struggle against sin, and to serve him faithfully. To fulfil these desires we shall find ourselves in need of much help, and we shall pray often, perhaps for our avenue of service, our Sunday School, or the effectiveness of our teaching. The result will be an experience of constant strengthening and blessing, and that will in turn assure our hearts, greatly uplifting us, and drawing us close to Christ.

Paul prays 'that Christ may dwell in your hearts *by faith*', the word *faith* meaning – being convinced or fully persuaded. Clearly if we are praying and receiving answers often we shall build up consider-able evidence of the goodness and power of God as he interacts with our lives. We shall be increasingly convinced, persuaded and certain that his promises are true, his Word is right, and that Christ Jesus is our glorious Lord and Saviour. It will become much harder for the devil or anyone on earth to persuade us that there is no God, no Christ, or that we are not truly converted. Paul's prayer, therefore, does not refer to rarefied sensations of ecstatic assurance imparted to us by God in a direct way (though, as we have said, special expe-riences may be given at times by the Lord). Paul's words speak of an assurance which is ours through experiencing the constant good-ness, power, comfort and consolation of the Lord in answer to our prayers.

For confirmation of this we note the opening words of Paul's doxology – 'Now unto him that is able to do exceeding abundantly above all that we ask or think, according to *the power that worketh in us*' *(Ephesians 3.20)*. The glorious knowledge of Christ in a personal and assured form is inextricably joined with the experience of prac-tical blessing.

Of course, this is not the whole story. Our study of the Word and our heartfelt worship also draw us close to Christ and build up assurance. We are increasingly assured as our minds are illuminated to grasp the deep things of the Word. Nevertheless, we must appreciate that much assurance flows from active involvement in the basic spiritual duties that we have reviewed, namely the sacrificial yielding of our time and energies in holiness and the service of the Lord. Some believers today seem to be saying, 'Oh, I do not want assurance this way. I do not want the duty of fighting against my sin. I do not want to renounce my leisure and be involved in Christian service. I want a direct blessing.' But how can Christ ever be entirely at home in such hearts? Why would the Holy Spirit give extraordinary blessings to those who want elevated feelings outside the normal duties of the Christian life?

The idea that believers can count on a direct form of assurance, unconnected with proving the Lord in the ways we have described, is so prevalent today that one has to prove the old doctrine many times over before the point is thoroughly received.

*Hebrews 6.11-12* emphasises this truth yet again. Here the Spirit of God states that assurance is obtained only by diligent application to spiritual duties. 'And we desire that every one of you do shew the same diligence to the full assurance of hope unto the end: that ye be not slothful, but followers of them who through faith and patience inherit the promises.'

Immediately before these verses the writer had referred to the Hebrews' 'work and labour of love'. They were zealous, earnest, striving, active believers, who proved the help of the Lord in their lives. The *NASB* renders the crucial statement very significantly: 'And we desire that each one of you show the same diligence so as to realize the full assurance of hope until the end.'

The apostle Peter adds his voice to the chorus of testimony that this is the chief pathway to assurance. In *2 Peter 1.5-8* there is a remarkable sequence of exhortations telling us to give all diligence to add to our faith virtue, and so on. Knowledge, self-control, patience, godliness, brotherly kindness and love all come into the list of things to which diligence must be applied. Then Peter gives a warning and a promise:

'But he that lacketh these things is blind, and cannot see afar off, and hath forgotten that he was purged from his old sins. Wherefore the rather, brethren, give diligence to make your calling and election sure:

for if ye do these things, ye shall never fall: for so an entrance shall be ministered unto you abundantly into the everlasting kingdom of our Lord and Saviour Jesus Christ' *(2 Peter 1.9-11).*

If we are not engaged in prayer for help and progress in the development of godly character and virtues then we will lose our spiritual 'sight' (though not, of course, our salvation). We shall feel lost and in darkness. We will even forget what it felt like when we were first pardoned and our hearts were lifted up in newborn happiness.

On the other hand, if we have a constant experience of answered prayer in the pursuit of practical holiness and service, then we shall never *fall* (which means 'stumble') into barrenness (v 8), fruitlessness or despondency. On the contrary, we shall *feel* like people who are entering into the kingdom.

If anyone has the slightest doubt that to co-operate with the Spirit in the quest for holiness and service is the major route to assurance, then the words of the apostle John will help. In *1 John 3.18-19* we read: 'My little children, let us not love in word, neither in tongue [only]; but in *deed* and in *truth*. And hereby we know that we are of the truth, and shall assure our hearts before him.'

*1 John* is, of course, very largely an epistle of assurance. John says – 'These things have I written unto you that believe on the name of the Son of God; that ye may know that ye have eternal life, and that ye may believe on the name of the Son of God' *(1 John 5.13).* Yet we go through *1 John* in vain to find any mention of a post-conversion baptism giving sensational feelings. This is not because John, writing under inspiration, denies that God may dispense direct assurance according to his own sovereign will and purpose, but because this epistle deals with the *practical* aspects of assurance. Therefore, John says with Paul: co-operate with the Spirit of God; pray for much help in your life; strive to advance in righteousness and to serve the Lord, and you will find that you receive so much evident help that you will gain solid encouragement, joy and certainty. Experiencing this means the living interaction of the Spirit in your life.

We have here laboured the point about a crucial and practical form of assurance strangely omitted from the teaching of most writers who advocate a baptism with the Spirit as the route to joy and certainty. However, this is not the only form of assurance, and we give the following list so that no form is overlooked.

(1) Assurance may be derived from consideration of the 'marks of grace' or signs of conversion given in the Scriptures. As we recognise that these have been experienced by us, and there is a divine work being carried on in our hearts, then we are gladdened and assured of our salvation.

(2) Assurance may be derived from a full and soul-warming view of Truth, as the Holy Spirit illuminates the mind in the reading of his Word, and as we feed upon the attributes, works and purposes of our glorious God.

(3) Evidential assurance (referred to chiefly just now in these pages) arises from the obvious strengthening, helping activity of the Spirit as the believer seeks prayerfully to live a sanctified life and serve the Lord, and also receives other glorious answers to prayer.

(4) Special assurance may be given, when the Holy Spirit from time to time gives such an unusually deep sense of assurance that the heart overflows in wonder, love and praise, and is taken up by a sense of the glory of God. Such assurance may be especially associated with times of persecution (as in the testimony of the noble army of martyrs), or grief, or special service for Christ. It is the Lord's doing, and it is very precious to the believer, but it is unscriptural to present it as the 'norm' to be sought after through a special baptism of the Spirit.

This writer has just read an article by a leading teacher advocating a post-conversion baptism of the Spirit, in which only two texts are taken, both being interpreted in an unorthodox and superficial way to prove the point. Most of the passages quoted in these last two chapters are not referred to. Sadly, this is characteristic of the teaching of post-conversion Spirit-baptism. The teachers abandon our rich tradition of exposition from past ages, including times of reformation and spiritual awakening, putting in their place poor interpretation of just a few verses taken out of context. In these pages we have sought to comb all the texts in order to be sure of the meaning of the infallible Word on this vital issue.

# 4
# The Spirit of Holiness

THE GREAT HERITAGE of doctrinal teaching reflected in the books of most commentators and preachers of the Reformation tradition holds that the development of believers in holiness is a progressive matter, involving their effort and co-operation with the work of the Holy Spirit in their lives. With the passage of time, however, a mystical stream of teaching arose claiming that just as we are *justified* by faith, so also we must be *sanctified* by faith. The idea is that a post-conversion baptism of the Spirit will take care of holiness, leaving us without the need for struggle and disappointment. This view was adopted by most Pentecostalists, so-called holiness and higher-life groups, and in more recent times by the majority of charismatics.

Before showing how the traditional route to sanctification differs from the Spirit-baptism, 'automatic sanctification' error, we again invite readers to take a brief look at some sentences from that famous and superb doctrinal summary, the *Baptist Confession of Faith of 1689* (also entitled, *Things Most Surely Believed Among Us*).

This is based on the *Westminster Confession of Faith*, and expresses the same teaching:–

> 'They who are united to Christ, effectually called, and regenerated, having a new heart and a new spirit created in them...are also farther sanctified, really and personally...by his Word and Spirit dwelling in them; the dominion of the whole body of sin is destroyed...'

We interrupt our quotation to point out how carefully the *Confession* writers express themselves. They do not say that the whole body of sin is destroyed, but that the *dominion* of the whole body of sin is destroyed. In other words, sin is still there, but it is no longer master of the life. To resume:–

> '...the dominion of the whole body of sin is destroyed, and the several lusts thereof are more and more weakened and mortified, and they *[believers]* more and more quickened and strengthened in all saving graces, to the practice of all true holiness, without which no man shall see the Lord.'

The *Confession* states very precisely that at conversion the *dominion* of sin is smashed and broken, but that the actual lusts or sinful desires are not caused to vanish. These are *progressively* weakened and put to death as believers advance in the practice of true holiness. Sanctification is described as a *progressive* work in the lives of believers.

The next paragraph in the *Confession* expands further on the existence of continuing sin (sometimes called 'residual' sin), and shows that the Spirit helps us to battle against it. Note the fighting language which is used:–

> 'This sanctification is throughout, in the whole man, yet imperfect in this life; there abideth still some remnants of corruption in every part, whence ariseth a continual and irreconcilable war; the flesh lusting against the Spirit, and the Spirit against the flesh.
> 'In which war, although the remaining corruption for a time may much prevail, yet, through the continual supply of strength from the sanctifying Spirit of Christ, the regenerate part doth overcome; and so the saints grow in grace, perfecting holiness in the fear of God, pressing after an heavenly life, in evangelical obedience to all the commands

which Christ, as Head and King, in his Word, hath prescribed to them.'

There is a fine comment on these statements in a book entitled, *The Westminster Confession Study Manual*, by G. I. Williamson:–

'The doctrine of sanctification...teaches us that there is rather a radical breach with the power and love of sin. It teaches us that established within us is a new power and love which necessitates unquenchable conflict with sin. The dominion of sin is broken, though the presence of sin is not entirely eliminated. Just as penicillin may break a fever, thus destroying the dominion of a disease, and yet some time elapses before every trace of the disease is eliminated, so it is with sin. Just as the Allied armies invaded Europe and destroyed the threat of Hitler's hope of world dominion, and yet required much more time to eradicate every vestige of it, so it is with sin.

'Sin no longer commands the heart. The main lines of communication have been destroyed. The control centre is now in the hands of God. But the alien force still carries on harassment of all kinds with all the skill, cunning and desperation of a defeated foe. As *[the late Professor John]* Murray has aptly said – there is a total difference between *surviving* sin and *reigning* sin.'

The great theologian John Owen, writing in 1652, expressed the way conversion alters the believer's relationship with sin in the following words:–

'By nature the flesh is wholly predominant constantly making the soul to sin. But when grace comes in, the habit of sin is weakened and impaired so that it shall not reign or lord it over us. But yet it is never entirely dispossessed and cast out of the soul in this life. There it will remain and work, seduce and tempt, more or less, according to its remaining strengths and advantages. Let no man think to kill sin with a few gentle strokes.'

Does all this mean that there are two natures in a Christian, the new nature which came in with conversion, and the old? There is only one predominant nature in the Christian, because the main disposition of the converted soul is to please God and to live for him and know him. Even in backslidden moments believers make ill-at-ease, unhappy worldlings. Our chief characteristic is that we love the Lord, and are 'on the Lord's side'. Yet if we use the term *nature* to describe any and all of our possible moods or states, then we have to say that there are two natures, because sin is still present in our lives. The Scriptures speak of the *old man* and the *new man*, saying the old has to be put off by believers, and the new put on *(Romans 6.6; Ephesians 4.22; Colossians 3.9)*. The old self (which some teachers prefer to call 'the flesh') is not entirely eradicated, and must be taken account of, and fought and defied.

There can be no victory over the old nature by the notion that we can obtain automatic sanctification by the Spirit, just by yielding to him, or receiving a 'second blessing' from him. This theory comes under a number of names today such as the victorious life, the higher Christian life, Christian perfection, entire sanctification, sanctification-by-faith, full-Gospel holiness, the faith-rest-life, the release of the Spirit, and scriptural brokenness, besides the baptism of the Spirit, the fulness of the Spirit, and the second blessing. Whatever this theory is called, it misrepresents the Scriptures. Many true believers have been persuaded that it is the right way, but the old nature (or the flesh) can never be banished or suppressed without a struggle. The theory of effortless, automatic holiness has disastrously failed countless believers, encouraging them to relax their vigilance and cease the constant battle against personal sin, causing them to fall into temptation and snares. Not only have standards of godliness fallen, and worldliness risen in the churches where these things are taught, but many people, imagining themselves to be on a higher spiritual plane, have been puffed up by pride.

Most 'traditional' pastors in recent decades have had the task at some time of having to bring reality into the lives of people who imagined they were filled with the Spirit and perfectly sanctified, when in fact they lived selfish, worldly lives. Adherents of these systems of Spirit-baptism often become highly subjective, and preoccupied with themselves and their supposed spiritual gifts, contrary to the unselfish, humble, outward-flowing serving spirit of true Christian character.

While noting the failure of these ideas to produce real holiness, we must have sympathy for their casualties. Numerous Christians have tried hard to obtain a post-conversion baptism of the Spirit to obtain holiness, but have failed to experience any of the promised phenomena or signs. For sincere people, the disappointment may lead to spiritual despair. They conclude that their failure to find the promised benefit is due to *their* faithless condition, and feel crushed and condemned.

Other believers have been influenced by bizarre forms of this kind of teaching, such as that which claims that the flesh is wrapped around the spirit, suffocating it, and what believers must do is humiliate and crack apart the flesh in order that the spirit may be released. This particular example of cult-like theology rose to amazing popularity among believers before World War II, and still has advocates. It produces intense introspection and anguish, especially in those who possess sensitive and vulnerable personalities.

The doctrine of sanctification of the Bible, so well explained by the Reformers and Puritans, and then by the great majority of sound preachers since, requires the believer to be actively involved in the struggle against sin, and by prayer and the strength imparted by the Spirit to mortify (put to death) sin. The words of the apostle stand: 'If ye through the Spirit do mortify the deeds of the body, ye shall live.'

# 5
## Attending the Wrong Classroom

I T GOES WITHOUT SAYING that the correct method of
seeking holiness must be that which is taught in the Bible.
But this leads to another issue – do we interpret the Bible in a
logical, sensible manner? Unfortunately, one of the chief character-
istics of Spirit-baptism teachers has been their unorthodox method
of handling the Bible. They usually support their ideas by quoting
verses which are wrested right out of their context and made to read
differently from their plain sense.

Many who promote the post-conversion baptism of the Spirit
think that their viewpoint does not have to be derived plainly and
directly from Scripture. They justify their novel interpretations on
the ground that they have received a special anointing of the Spirit
to grasp the real but often half-hidden meaning of the passages
they quote, a meaning which other Christians fail to see (they say)
because they do not have a special illumination of the Holy Spirit.
Naturally, as soon as we accept this 'special anointing' notion, then
we have numerous different 'Bibles', and we lose our sure yardstick

of Truth. The Word of God ceases to be a clear authority and rule for believers, because it depends upon something incapable of being tested and verified – individual 'anointing'.

We believe that an anointing of the Spirit is essential for the understanding of Scripture, but this comes with the powerful work of conversion in our souls, so that we become *spiritual* rather than *natural* people. The apostle John, in *1 John 2.27*, indicates that this anointing is in every believer, not just 'special' people, and that it abides with them all the time. Furthermore it does not impart to us meanings that cannot be seen in the text.

After conversion we continue to need the help of God, and we therefore pray for humility and discernment as we study the Scripture, but there is no peculiar kind of anointing which gives any believer an entirely unique and personal view of a passage, concealed from others. In the study of the Bible we are obliged to follow the Bible's own rules of interpretation. We consider first the plain and obvious sense of the passage. We then take care to relate the passage to its context. We compare our interpretation with other scriptures on the same subject, lest we should arrive at a conclusion which makes Scripture contradict itself. In controversial matters particularly we carefully check the meaning of words in the orig-inal languages of Scripture. And we also pay respectful attention to trustworthy teachers and commentators before jumping to novel conclusions.[*]

It has to be said that even the most noted exponents of post-conversion Spirit-baptism and automatic sanctification usually work in disregard of these basic interpretive rules. If they were to respect them, their teaching would collapse instantly.

Here is a major example of the kind of mistake they make by ignoring the basic rules of logical interpretation. These teachers

---

[*] See *Not Like Any Other Book*, chapter 11, 'Positive Steps of Interpretation', Peter Masters, Wakeman Trust, London.

constantly use texts dealing with *justification*, to teach the principles of *sanctification*. At school or college, it makes sense to attend the right lecture. It will not help to go to the lecture room designated for chemistry if the student's subject is physics. If, by some absurdity, a student goes into the wrong class and tries to accommodate the lecture to his subject, his confusion will be nothing short of spectacular. Yet here is the strange mistake made by all the teachers of sanctification-by-faith. To get their sanctification data, they go into Scripture passages about justification. Consider how they explain *Galatians 2.20.* Paul says: 'I am crucified with Christ: nevertheless I live; yet not I, but Christ liveth in me: and the life which I now live in the flesh I live by the faith of the Son of God, who loved me, and gave himself for me.'

They use this verse to teach that in order to live holy lives we must die to ourselves in the sense that we must give up all personal effort to resist sin, depending instead on Christ to manifest his power and life in us, and to entirely take over the battle. To 'die', in their interpretation, is to give up the struggle. But the verse is not about ongoing sanctification. As soon as we check the context (the subject of the surrounding verses) we find that the whole passage is about *justification*. It is about salvation. Being *justified* is mentioned three times in the preceding verses. Paul is refuting people who taught justification by works, and asserting the necessity of *justifying* righteousness (not sanctifying righteousness). Sanctification-by-faith teachers have gone into the wrong lecture room, and consulted the wrong text.

*Galatians 2.20* is probably the chief anchor of automatic-sanctification teachers, and yet it has been used illegitimately. The subject is *justification* by faith alone right through *Galatians 1, 2, 3* and *4.* Only then does Paul turn his attention to holy living, in chapter five.

In their manner of interpretation the automatic-sanctification teachers range from the careless to the bizarre. They seem unaware of their constant misuse of God's Word, wrenching it to fit their opinions. And they go on using *justification* verses to teach *sanctification* theories. As this matter is so important, a quick review of the first two chapters of *Galatians* must be made. In *Galatians 1.6* the apostle states clearly that his subject is – 'another gospel', so he is clearly speaking about salvation or justification. Then in *Galatians 2.4-5* the apostle mentions false brethren (Judaisers) who sneaked into the churches in order to plot against the doctrine of justification by faith alone.

In *Galatians 2.11* we note that Peter yielded to these Judaising brethren and had to be withstood by Paul. This chapter is brimming over with the subject of justification – defending it, explaining it, insisting upon it. So *Galatians 2.20* speaks of how we must be freed from the law and *justified*, about how we are made clean in the sight of God. The apostle states that it is by being crucified with Christ. It is our sin, our guilt, our 'old life' which is crucified with Christ. When, therefore, the apostle says in *Galatians 2.20*, 'Nevertheless I live; yet not I, but Christ liveth in me,' he is undoubtedly speaking about the result of justification. Once justified, to live is to walk with Christ, so that Christ now has an interest in me, his plans and purposes are now being worked out in me, and I am his property. I have received a new principle of life in me, with new tastes and enjoyments, and I am bound for Heaven. *Galatians 2.20* is the fruit of being justified by faith. There is no intention on the part of the apostle to teach or imply a *by-faith* method of achieving holiness (which would contradict all the exhortations to effort which he proceeds to give in *Galatians 5* and *6*).

In the study of these passages the differences between *justification* and *sanctification* must always be observed. *Justification* is the matter of being pardoned and declared righteous (solely and entirely through Christ), whereas *sanctification* is the process of being *made* righteous. *Justification* is something which takes place once and for ever at conversion. *Sanctification*, on the other hand, is continuous and progressive and will not be finally completed until we go to Heaven. *Justification* is achieved absolutely and entirely by God alone, but in *sanctification* the Holy Spirit both inspires and enables the believer's own striving after holiness.

# 6
## Are We to Fight Sin?

**H**OW IS IT that many Bible-reading Christians fail to see the fighting-striving language of the New Testament? Think of Paul's words in *Ephesians 6.13*: 'Wherefore take unto you the whole armour of God, that ye may be able to withstand in the evil day, and having done all, to stand.' The first truth to be noted in this passage is that *there is a battle to be fought*, and while it must be fought with the armour and weapons provided by the Lord, the battle will be fought by the person who wears the armour and wields the sword. The passage names several items of military equipment which must be personally taken up and used, every piece being vital. No single act (such as seeking a baptism of the Spirit) can take the place of the several duties which the Scripture lays upon us. All the accoutrements of spiritual warfare are needed, because the devil is so subtle. Throughout the New Testament the words for sanctification are all fighting terms – *mortify, crucify, strive, wrestle,* and *fight*.

Another passage on this subject is *Philippians 2.12-13*, where Paul says, 'Work out your own salvation with fear and trembling.

For it is God which worketh in you both to will and to do of his good pleasure.' At a casual glance there seems to be a contradiction between the two halves of this quotation. One moment the apostle tells us to work out our own salvation with fear and trembling, and the next he tells us that it is God who works in us. But obviously the apostle would not contradict himself within a few words. He commands us to strive for holiness and obedience, explaining that it is the Spirit's method to stiffen our *will* to strive, and increase our *strength* to succeed. The Spirit does not bypass our efforts (as the automatic-sanctification teachers imagine), but gives us the desire and determination to advance. We could paraphrase Paul's words thus: 'For it is God who works in you, bringing your will to desire his way, and bringing your motives, desires and actions to be entirely aligned to his pleasure.'

We could marshal very many passages from the epistles to show that the apostle always urged believers to engage *personally* and *directly* in the battle against sin. The struggle for holiness is an unavoidable experience for the believer. It cannot be bypassed or handed over to the Lord. To engage in this conflict is an absolute duty, and we are promised the ever-present help and power of the Holy Spirit.

In *Galatians 5.16-17*, for example, Paul tells us plainly about the battle: 'This I say then, Walk in the Spirit, and ye shall not fulfil the lust of the flesh. For the flesh lusteth against the Spirit, and the Spirit against the flesh: and these are contrary the one to the other: so that ye cannot do the things that ye would.' As we might expect, Spirit-baptism writers derive from these verses a variety of meanings which one would never see without their ingenious twists of interpretation. Some say that these verses teach the hopelessness of engaging in the battle against sin. They insist that taking up the fight ourselves will lead to impossible turmoil and failure. Instead we should concentrate on our communion with the Holy Spirit and with Christ, and then the Lord will look after our holiness.

But the plain sense of the passage (and the interpretation given by the overwhelming majority of Bible commentators) is as follows. Because we are Christians, our old, sinful self is in conflict with our new, Spirit-indwelt nature. If we walk spiritually, praying for help, then the battle will become *even more intense,* because the Holy Spirit will wake up our consciences so that temptations and sinful desires will cause us great pain and discomfort, making it hard for us to sin. The Holy Spirit will ring the alarm bells of conscience, then we will have to play our part in responding to these alarms. As soon as we proceed to yield to temptation and indulge in sin, pangs of conscience will hold us back. If we resent the voice of conscience, suppress its challenge, and resist its pressure, then we 'trample' not only on conscience, but also on the Spirit. If we justify our sin and stifle these spiritual instincts, then the Holy Spirit will be grieved, our hearts will grow hard and cold, our consciences rendered insensible, and sin will revive within us. If, however, we respond to the challenge of conscience and cry out to God to help us, we will be strengthened to resist and defeat the temptation.

The struggle within us is irksome and sometimes painful, but it is life and health to our souls. There is work for us to do in this battle, as the apostle constantly shows. Why are there so many exhortations and commands to holiness in the Bible if it is not necessary for us to obey them?

In *Galatians 6* the first six verses contain positive, practical duties which the believer is commanded to carry out personally. These are called sowing to the Spirit *(Galatians 6.8).* The fact is that *we* must do these things. In other words, the battle against sin, and the struggle to obey the Lord, cannot be avoided. May no reader be confused by any of the incredible theories and teachings about holiness proposed by sanctification-by-faith teachers.

# 7
# Must We Be Emptied or Broken?

A PARTICULARLY bizarre aspect of the post-conversion
baptism view taught by many among its adherents is the
idea that our 'personhood' must be constantly torn out
and crucified afresh in order to attain to holiness. The real *you*, they
insist, is apparently unchanged, unhallowed and untouched by the
new birth. It is all bad and it must be utterly broken and thrown
away.

But the Scriptures say that God is working in us to do something
far greater than that. His plan is to cause the new person to *want*
and to *will* the right things. The Bible teaches that God is working
in us to progressively sanctify the heart which was renewed at
conversion, not to tear it out and replace it. Grace first transforms us
and then progressively refines us. The mystical-holiness movement
takes away from God his right and power to *change* Christians from
glory to glory. It virtually says that nothing can alter or improve
humanity – not even conversion. We can only be sanctified by being
depersonalised and entirely taken over by the Spirit. If any small

grain of us continues to exist, the battle will be lost. Only if we become completely empty vessels can any victory occur. This is the teaching of so many charismatic and holiness groups.

This concept is the exact opposite of what is taught in the Scriptures, where we see ourselves as *transformed* children of God, equipped by the new birth with spiritual faculties and a measure of power over sin. Certainly we continue to need the mighty power of God, and we will fall if we proceed alone, but the reality is that, unworthy as we are, we *are* different, and already partially empowered for the fight against sin. The Word of God says:

> 'But ye are a chosen generation, a royal priesthood, an holy nation, a peculiar people; that ye should shew forth the praises of him who hath called you out of darkness into his marvellous light: which in time past were not a people, but are now the people of God: which had not obtained mercy, but now have obtained mercy' *(1 Peter 2.9-10).*

We are to appreciate our 'status' as sons and members of the heavenly family. We are not saved to be zombies, puppets, robots or empty vessels. It is crucial to realise that in sanctification God deals with us as children, but the mystical-holiness system of sanctification misses this point entirely. God deals with us, according to the Scripture, as beloved and privileged sons and daughters. At conversion he remakes us to be fully equipped with the Word to fulfil his will *(2 Timothy 3.16-17).* It is his purpose that each of his children should voluntarily strive to please and serve him with their own born-again faculties, directed by Scripture *plus* the mighty help of the Spirit. At conversion (the only true baptism of the Spirit) the Holy Spirit gives us a new life, with new faculties and a new nature, and this is not something to be broken as though it were utterly hopeless.

Any system of sanctification which claims that the only way to be sanctified is to be emptied and to become 'nothing at all', has completely misunderstood the glorious teaching of the Word. Yet mystical-holiness teachers constantly insist that we can only be sanctified as we renounce all effort and accept that we have no contribution to make.

God has given us many precious powers and privileges. To tear down or disregard the transforming work which took place at conversion, and to convince ourselves that we are hopeless, worthless, powerless, empty vessels is to go far beyond the humble recognition of our continuing weaknesses and sinfulness. It is to despise what God has done for us. Our sanctification involves our *voluntarily* serving him more, loving him more, and undertaking service for him. We are to use the new faculties which he has given us as sons and heirs, and we are to love and serve him with all our heart, and all our soul, and all our strength, and all our mind, as the Word commands us to do. The notions of charismatic and mystical-holiness teachers constantly conflict with the language of God's Word. They are strange and peculiar ideas which should be rejected and avoided by Christian people.

# 8
# The Filling of the Spirit

T HERE IS AN OLD SAYING, 'One baptism; many fillings.' The biblical position, we believe, is that the only baptism of the Holy Spirit is that which occurs in connection with regeneration, at conversion. Whether we choose to call it a baptism *with* the Spirit, or a baptism *of* the Spirit, the Bible makes clear, as we have seen, that it is one and the same baptism, and it occurs at conversion. However, there is in the New Testament a further blessing by the Spirit which is called the *filling* of the Spirit, and this may happen on more than one occasion in the life of an earnest Christian, even often.

This is nothing like the additional baptism of the Spirit which Pentecostalists, charismatics and higher-life teachers say we must have after conversion. Their baptism is a claimed ecstatic experience, usually accompanied by various physical sensations, and by what are described as tongues, although usually they are not literal languages as in the Bible. Most of their teachers say (as we have seen) that through this baptism the Spirit completely takes over from us the work of sanctification. Others emphasise more the idea that heightened feelings of assurance, glory and communion with God come through this baptism.

However, the *filling* of the Spirit, which is mentioned a number of times in *Acts*, is quite different in character and purpose from such a 'baptism'. To discover the nature of this filling, we will first list eight references to it in *Acts*.

*Acts 2.4.* On the Day of Pentecost all the disciples were filled.

*Acts 4.8.* Peter gave his defence before the high priests, and was filled with the Spirit.

*Acts 4.31-32.* The disciples were filled again with the Spirit in answer to their prayer. They asked for, and received, great boldness. They also received a spirit of oneness and love.

*Acts 6.3.* The filling of the Spirit was regarded as a qualification for the first diaconate. Spiritual wisdom and holiness of life indicated this filling.

*Acts 7.55.* Stephen was filled with the Spirit and given grace for martyrdom.

*Acts 9.17.* Paul was filled following his conversion, thereby being prepared to stand up to the sufferings which God was about to show him (see *Acts 9.15-16*), and for his new role (vv 19-20).

*Acts 13.9.* The Holy Spirit filled Paul again in preparation for his work, and granted him discernment and boldness.

*Acts 13.52.* The disciples of Pisidian Antioch were given great joy and assurance when they were filled with the Spirit. They were strengthened to witness in a difficult place in the midst of persecution.

As we study these references we realise that the same people were sometimes present at more than one filling. They were therefore filled more than once, at different times and for different objectives.

The purpose of these fillings is clear from the circumstances of the recipients, and the effects which they had. A filling of the Spirit produced boldness, effectiveness in witness, great love, unity of purpose, deep commitment to the Lord's work (seen in the stewardship of all their goods), wisdom, discernment, spiritual comfort in persecution, assurance and also joy. We notice that these fillings of the Spirit are usually referred to in terms of their *results*, and never in terms of how it felt to be filled.

The very earliest filling was accompanied by the amazing sign of speaking in real foreign languages (not like the mere glossolalia of present-day tongues-speaking), so that the disciples preached to Jews in the different languages of the regions from which they came. None of the other filling references include tongues-speaking, contrary to the careless claims of many writers.*

The apostle Paul also refers to the filling of the Spirit in *Ephesians 5.18* – a chapter about self-control, holiness and wise behaviour. He tells us that a filling of the Spirit is to be sought to accomplish these objectives. The filling, then, is a very practical benefit which empowers believers (in *Acts*) to witness, preach, sacrifice, steward and love, and also (in *Ephesians*) to lead a holy life.

It is surely significant that in *Acts* the filling was never asked for in name by those who received it. There is no indication that they ever prayed for it by name. They certainly prayed for the power and help of God to accomplish various things (eg: *Acts 4.29*), but although they did not specifically ask for it, what they received was a filling of the Spirit. In other words, the filling of the Spirit was not an experience which was to be sought *for its own sake*. Nor are we told in *Acts* that it involved any felt sensations of any kind. (These are the inventions of over-imaginative teachers.) The only *feelings* we can connect to a filling of the Spirit (from studying the *Acts* references) are those of joy and love. Doubtless also the disciples felt strongly assured, because they received power and boldness. There is

---

* The only two other occurrences of tongues-speaking in *Acts* (besides *Acts 2*) are in *Acts 10.46* and *Acts 19.6*. These, as we show in chapter 11, were not fillings of the Spirit, but outpourings, serving as 'miniature Pentecosts'.

certainly no mention of feelings such as tingling sensations up and down the spine, or waves of heat, or ecstasies, or of strange power, or involuntary lifting of the arms. Nothing physical is referred to or hinted at in the entire record of fillings. No one ever broke out in uncontrolled shouting, or lay prostrate on the ground weeping and calling out. Present-day charismatics and second-blessing writers claim a long list of extraordinary sensations which are not to be seen anywhere in the New Testament. In *Acts* and *Ephesians* the filling of the Spirit is always a practical empowering, and not an ecstatic experience. These fillings all had a *definite, practical result.*

Today there are people who seek an experience of the Spirit purely for some personal, sensational kick. They want a wonderful experience, or they want to be exempted from the battle against sin. You hear them say, 'I want God's best for me.' But there is nothing like that in the Word of God. A filling of the Spirit is always given with a practical, holy objective.

We note also that the practical result of the filling of the Spirit was to give the disciples power to *do* something, not to have it entirely done for them. Every single filling in the New Testament empowered, prepared or helped the disciples to *do* something extremely hard. There is no scope for the unscriptural catchphrase 'Let go, let God!' in the fillings of the *Book of Acts.*

This brings us to the ideal scripture for giving balance and perspective about the Holy Spirit and his wonderful work in our hearts. Neither baptism nor filling is mentioned, yet the sharing of the believer's effort and the Spirit's enabling is perfectly set out. The verse appears at the end of *2 Corinthians*, 'The grace of the Lord Jesus Christ, and the love of God, and the communion of the Holy Ghost, be with you all' *(2 Corinthians 13.14).*

The *communion* or partnership of the Holy Spirit is the amazing kindness and condescension of the Spirit whereby he 'stoops down to us and enfolds us in his communion' (the words of R. C. H. Lenski). It is the Holy Spirit who imparts to us the blessings of our salvation, bringing us into the family of the redeemed. Whatever Christ has secured for us, the Holy Spirit applies to our lives, and through him we become sharers; partners of spiritual life itself.

But the word *communion* or partnership explains a vital principle which sanctification-by-faith teachers entirely pass by. This school of opinion insists that unless the Holy Spirit possesses and fills every part and crevice of our being (leaving absolutely nothing of *us*) we cannot possibly be sanctified. We have seen already that by this theory of sanctification the Lord really accomplishes nothing at all in the lives of his people, but rather makes them empty shells, the Spirit himself substituting, rather than refining, their faculties. There is no *sharing*, no *partnership* at all, only disposal of the person, and a complete takeover.

The correct concept is that God's grace takes vile sinners, freely converts them by faith alone, and then gradually perfects them as saints by causing them to strive for holiness. This can be accomplished because the Holy Spirit shares himself with us and shares the task with us.

The Holy Spirit does not smash us and take us over. He imparts his life into ours and brings us to participate in the process of sanctification. He does not eclipse us, and take away all our identity and responsibility. He comes alongside to equip and empower us. He is a *partner*, even in the business sense of the word.

Someone may aim at running a small business, a shop perhaps, but not have the necessary capital. A wealthy friend provides the funds and becomes a partner. There would be no business without the partner, but he does not engage in the day-to-day labour of the business. He does not arrive in the morning to open the shop, remove the shutters, put out the goods, or operate the till. The *active* partner performs all these things, while the sponsor provides capital and counsel. The illustration is far from perfect, but the Holy Spirit is a *partner* to us. Whenever more capital is needed by way of power and guidance, we turn to our infinitely rich and powerful partner, for we are entirely dependent upon him for wherewithal and counsel. The relationship is a *partnership*, or sharing, which is the exact sense of the Greek word translated 'communion'.

When the apostle Paul prays that the *communion* of the Holy Ghost may be with us all, he reminds us that we depend on the Holy Spirit for our power, and also that there is much for us to do in the pursuit of sanctification.

Numerous charismatic and sanctification-by-faith teachers insist that *Ephesians 5.18* proves that our own identity must be displaced in every respect by the occupation of the Spirit. 'And be not drunk with wine, wherein is excess; but be filled with the Spirit.' But this verse does not say that to receive a filling of the Spirit we must first totally empty ourselves, looking to the Holy Spirit to do everything for us.

The Greek *filling* word is used many times in the New Testament. It is used, for example, in *Romans 11.25*, where Paul speaks of the 'fulness of the Gentiles' having come in. Does he mean that all those who had been saved during Old Testament times would be eradicated to make way for the Gentiles? Of course not. The *filling* word as used here does not imply a prior emptying. He means *completion* or topping up, not emptying and filling.

In *Romans 15.14* the apostle Paul commends the Romans for being 'filled with all knowledge'. Did he mean that they now knew everything? Of course not. The filling word does not necessarily imply either complete emptying, or absolute fulness.

A similar reference is found in *Ephesians 3.19*, where the apostle prays that they might be 'filled with all the fulness of God'. This, of course, is impossible, and reading the verse no reasonable person thinks that the Ephesians could be completely filled with all the infinite being of Almighty God. We must understand the words *filled* and *filling* in a less than fully literal way.

If we fill a jug with water, it does not necessarily mean that we throw away the water already in it. We simply fill it up. The *filling* of the Spirit does not totally scrap everything that has been put in the believer at conversion. It means that the Spirit makes up our deficiencies, giving power where we are weak, wisdom where we are ignorant or naive, and courage where we are cowardly.

So the exhortation to seek always the empowering (filling) of the Spirit (in *Ephesians 5.18*) is completely consistent with that final verse in *2 Corinthians*, which presents the Holy Spirit as being in communion or partnership with us. As we strive for holiness, *he* blesses with power. The aim of the Spirit is to build holiness and service in *our* lives, not to replace our personhood with his own. Conversion bestows upon us a range of gifts, strengths and abilities, and these are to be purified and dedicated to God, not resigned or discarded.

A genuine filling of the Spirit is the invisible empowering of the Spirit which strengthens and enables us whenever we sincerely and humbly cry out to God for help. We should begin every day by recognising our need of help for holiness, for witness and for the Lord's service, and as we do so, praying for strength, fluency and boldness, we will receive the enabling filling of the Spirit of God.

# *9*
# The Spirit's Way

PREVIOUS PAGES have set out the Scripture passages proving that the Holy Spirit does not sanctify by a special baptism, or by taking over the battle, but by convicting and stirring the hearts of believers, and then by strengthening them. This work of sanctification begins from the time of conversion (the occurrence of the one and only *baptism* of the Spirit), and is carried out through a range of means. The Spirit's ways are set out in this chapter, though the order is not intended to convey any scale of importance.

## 1. Faith

First, the Holy Spirit sanctifies by *our faith*, for we read in *Ephesians 6.16*: 'Above all, taking the shield of faith, wherewith ye shall be able to quench all the fiery darts *[temptations to sin or to doubt]* of the wicked.' Obviously, this does not mean that we are sanctified by faith in the sense that the Spirit-baptism teachers claim, that is, that the Spirit does it all. Faith operates in sanctification because, as we trust in the power and promises of God, we become –

(a) more eager to obey and honour God, and

(b) strengthened to do so.

When we really believe that our sovereign God is watching over us, we inevitably behave better, and we are also helped to endure sufferings and setbacks without self-pity, bitterness, jealousy, and spite. While we keep a strong trust in our Saviour, and keep his promises in view, we also avoid falling into the slough of despond.

When the allurements of this passing world are presented to us, and we are tempted to desire worldly things, or to yield to worldly ambitions, then our faith and trust in God's plan and purpose checks us and holds us safe. We remember that this is a vain and fallen world which can never be trusted, and the saying of *1 John 5.4* is fulfilled in our experience – 'For whatsoever is born of God overcometh the world: and this is the victory that overcometh the world, even our faith.'

Equally, our faith is the shield which protects us from the lies which the devil whispers to us in his campaign to steal our assurance and our joy and peace.

Faith enables us to live as people who owe a great debt to the Saviour. As we remember our merciful deliverance from sin and death, and all the blessings which are ours, we become ashamed of our sinfulness, and we reason in the same way as Paul, who said, 'We are debtors, not to the flesh, to live after the flesh . . . For I reckon that the sufferings of this present time are not worthy to be compared with the glory which shall be revealed in us' *(Romans 8.12 and 18)*.

Faith, hope and love go together, and when we keep our faith alive, we are full of gratitude and love for the Lord. We gladly set our affections on things above, not on things on the earth *(Colossians 3.2)*, and we are spurred to conscientious effort to please him by godly living.

Where does our faith come from? It comes obviously from the Holy Spirit, who first imparted it to us at conversion – the only baptism of the Spirit.

## 2. The Word of God

A second principal method of bringing about advance in sanctification, by the Spirit, is the *right use of the Word of God*. Every believer is familiar with Paul's words in *2 Timothy 3.16*: 'All scripture is given by inspiration of God, and is profitable for doctrine, for reproof, for correction, for instruction in righteousness.'

God's Word will sometimes *reprove* us so that we have to put matters right, either in our lives or in our church conduct. It will *correct* us, so that we modify our ways when we have drifted off course. It will *instruct* us, so that we become equipped to carry out every good work. We must allow the Scriptures to challenge us.

We note that Timothy is told that in preaching this Word he should 'reprove, rebuke, exhort with all longsuffering and doctrine' *(2 Timothy 4.2)*. The pulpit is to apply the Word of God, so that it speaks to shape the conduct and challenge the errors of believers. Through the Word, whether read privately or preached, we fulfil the desire of the Lord expressed in his prayer for his people *(John 17.17)* – 'Sanctify them through thy truth: thy word is truth.'

The Word of God is obviously a chief means of sanctification as it challenges, provokes and exhorts the people of God. But do we have the right level of awe and respect for the Word to respond to it? Many people talk much about their baptism of the Spirit, and about their amazing experiences and words of knowledge and so on, but they fail to obey even the basic commands of God's authoritative Word. What kind of Spirit-baptism is that? The promoters of Spirit-baptism around the world include some of the teachers most notorious for ignoring the rules and standards of God's Word. We see this in their worldliness: their love of worldly pleasures and use of distinctly worldly music, and the way they pervert worship to please these tastes. True spiritual life and obedience is to be seen in a person's love, awe and reverence for the Word, and obedience to its teaching.

# 3. Special dedication

A third route to sanctification is to be seen in *special acts of commitment or dedication*. We could refer to a large number of scriptures to establish the great value of acts of special dedication, but perhaps the most obvious is *Romans 12*. In verse one Paul writes: 'I beseech you therefore, brethren, by the mercies of God, that ye present your bodies a living sacrifice, holy, acceptable unto God, which is your reasonable service.'

It may be said that this is a standard for Christians all the time, and this is certainly true. But Paul seems here to call us to renew our vows in a special act of dedication, using in his exhortation the language of an act of sacrifice. We are not just to drift along in the Christian life, satisfied with only general and vague aspirations to be more committed to the Lord. From time to time we are to take ourselves in hand and make a definite recommitment of ourselves. We need to review every department of our activity, and then give ourselves up to the Lord afresh, together with our time, energy and resources; indeed with everything we are and have. The regular practice of rededication is the highest fulfilment of *Romans 12*.

An act of dedication may take a negative form, as when the children of Israel were told to keep apart from 'the accursed thing' *(Joshua 6.18)*. Achan disobeyed and took the forbidden spoil, bringing disaster to his family. Holiness involves obedience to God in remaining apart from things which God condemns. The well-known words of *2 Corinthians 6.17* command separation from unrighteousness and idolatry – 'Wherefore come out from among them, and be ye separate, saith the Lord, and touch not the unclean thing; and I will receive you.' We are to have nothing to do with evil, with worldliness, or with false religious teachers, who spurn the infallible Word of God, and teach error in the name of Christ. Our love for the Lord and for his Word should lead us to obey God's call.

Amazingly, those who claim super-spiritual baptisms are often among the most unseparated and disobedient of those who claim the name of Christ. Throughout the world the vast majority of charismatic leaders are in close alliance with apostate denominations and false teachers. Very many advocate unity of Bible believers with non-evangelicals such as the Roman Catholic church, their declared ultimate desire being a worldwide church headed by the pope. How can they possibly be 'baptised' and 'filled' with the Holy Spirit of Truth, when he, in the Word, commands that born-again people must never join themselves with error?

## 4. Mortifying of sin

A fourth (constantly operating) method of sanctification is that of mortifying or *putting to death* our sinful ways by the help of the Spirit. The principal scriptures in which we are exhorted to put to death the deeds of the body, or to 'deny' them or 'cleanse' them, are: *Romans 8.13; Colossians 3.5; Romans 6.12-13; 2 Corinthians 7.1;* and *Titus 2.11-12.* The first two of these passages read as follows:–

> 'For if ye live after the flesh, ye shall die: but if ye through the Spirit do mortify the deeds of the body, ye shall live.'
>
> 'Mortify therefore your members which are upon the earth; fornication, uncleanness, inordinate affection, evil concupiscence, and covetousness...'

Progress in sanctification is bound up with the activity of personally putting to death, contradicting or rejecting the sinful desires of the body, wrong speaking, and the temptations of the devil, together with the lifestyles, fashions and allurements of the world. Mortifying the deeds of the body is an activity which *we* must carry out, praying to the Lord for his powerful help.

In sanctification, our wills should be committed to this task, so that we live throughout our lives in thoughtful, intelligent, active opposition to sin. We put up a battle, an opposition, a constant resistance to the desires of the flesh. Paul tells us in *Romans 6.12-13,* that sanctification is a matter of refusing to allow our bodily faculties, passions and parts to serve sin, and instead, consciously yielding them to do righteous deeds. In the light of such strong texts, all ideas of automatic sanctification, or of handing the battle over to the Lord and doing nothing, are foolish, cult-like notions.

## 5. Chastening of the Lord

A fifth means of sanctification is the *chastening of the Lord*, referred to in *Hebrews 12.5-6* where the writer says: 'My son, despise not thou the chastening of the Lord, nor faint when thou art rebuked of him: for whom the Lord loveth he chasteneth, and scourgeth every son whom he receiveth.' We are not to resent or resist this chastening when it occurs in our lives. We see in these verses a twofold discipline – the *chastening* and the *rebuke*, the *chastening* being the more gentle of the two, sometimes ignored or disregarded (despised) on that account. The *rebuke* is clearly much more severe, because when it comes we are inclined to 'faint' and feel resentment or self-pity. So we see a carefully directed, fatherly discipline, moving from mild to firm, bringing us to our senses when we go wrong.

A still more severe form of discipline is seen in *1 Corinthians 11.30*: 'For this cause many are weak and sickly among you, and many sleep.' Some believers evidently had to be very severely judged because of their lack of self-examination, repentance and reform. They had lost their concern to lead sanctified lives, and God had chastised them. The apostle says, 'For if we would judge ourselves, we should not be judged.'

The significant point about chastening is that it is a process of love, from the Father to his child. 'God dealeth with you as with sons,' says *Hebrews 12.7*, 'for what son is he whom the father chasteneth not?' The Lord has an ongoing programme of infinitely wise (and no doubt as gentle as possible) chastisement for the training of his children when they stray from the mark. It is not enjoyable (contrary to the 'happy-all-the-day' ideas of Spirit-baptism teachers), but it leads to peace and righteousness in the case of 'them which are exercised' by it *(Hebrews 12.11)*. It is the indwelling Holy Spirit's work to bring us to the point where we eventually respond meekly, rather than bitterly, to such chastisement. By no means all sickness and suffering is a form of chastisement, much of it being a means of blessing for us, as our next section of the chapter will show.

# 6. Sickness and Suffering

A sixth means of bringing about our sanctification is *suffering and sickness*, which God uses to train and develop patience and faith.

While the Lord often heals in answer to prayer, it may be that a believer is called to endure a period of sickness, through which the Lord will deepen prayer, spiritual knowledge and experience. Paul testifies to this in *2 Corinthians 12.9* where he tells us that God declined to heal him, saying, 'My grace is sufficient for thee: for my strength is made perfect in weakness.' Paul's response was, 'Most gladly therefore will I rather glory in my infirmities, that the power of Christ may rest upon me.' Trials also contribute to our witness, for others see that we have a very real grip on divine help, and a wonderful source of comfort and joy.

There are many benefits and purposes to sickness, and sanctification is certainly one of them. Such trials lead God's people to self-examination and review of their lives; cause them to consider their frailty and dependence upon God's power; and stir them to think of the future, and to review their commitment to the Lord's service. Sickness frequently gives time for more prayer, communion, and intercession for others.

In sickness, souls become more important than bodies, Heaven more important than earth, and bringing pleasure to the Lord more important than pleasing self.

In sickness, believers often gain higher and deeper views of the Lord than at any other time, grasping more of his omnipotence and infinite holiness.

How often it has been said that sickness is the believer's

second-best blessing after health, and so it should be, for 'all things work together for good to them that love God' *(Romans 8.28)*.

What is it that makes sickness a lighthouse of Truth and a fountain of pleasure to a believer, when it is all horror to an unbeliever? Is it a special baptism of the Spirit? No, it is the work of the mighty, loving Holy Spirit who dwells within every true believer from the time of conversion. By *his* grace and goodness, we may walk through the very darkest valleys of life's journey, so that they become places of spiritual experience and advance.

## 7. Mutual admonition

A seventh means of our sanctification is the *practice of mutual admonition* among the Lord's people. Four scriptures (out of many) may be quoted to prove this duty – *Romans 15.14, Colossians 3.16, Galatians 6.1* and *James 5.19-20*:

> 'And I myself also am persuaded of you, my brethren, that ye also are full of goodness, filled with all knowledge, able also to admonish one another.'
>
> 'Let the word of Christ dwell in you richly in all wisdom; teaching and admonishing one another.'
>
> 'Brethren, if a man be overtaken in a fault, ye which are spiritual, restore such an one in the spirit of meekness; considering thyself, lest thou also be tempted.'
>
> 'Brethren, if any of you do err from the truth, and one convert him; let him know, that he which converteth the sinner from the error of his way shall save a soul from death, and shall hide a multitude of sins.'

The ministry of mutual admonition is of incalculable value, but it is an activity which is possible only where believers are truly close to each other in spiritual oneness and friendship, and where they are able to admonish with true humility and grace. The Lord will certainly use us to contribute to one another's progress in sanctification. This is another method of sanctification not included in the ideas of the advocates of Spirit-baptism and automatic sanctification. The fact is, however, that the Lord sets believers in families (churches), and the Spirit, who indwells them from conversion, uses them to minister to one another by encouragement, warning and friendly exhortation.

## Conclusion

These seven routes or ways by which the Spirit sanctifies depend upon his superintendency of our circumstances, and his silent work in our hearts. It is the Holy Spirit who makes us receptive to various correcting, shaping influences. He works in such a way that we freely, willingly and personally strive to advance, praying for his help.

# 10
## A Baptism of Bliss?

**M**ANY ADVOCATES of a post-conversion baptism of the Spirit insist that Spirit-filled Christians are not only automatically made holy, but are also continuously happy and even healthy. They promise an uninterrupted enjoyment of the power and presence of Christ as long as the believer 'abides in Christ' and 'walks in the Spirit'. The classic example of this idea is to be seen in *How to Live the Victorious Life* – the anonymous best-seller which has presented this point of view over several decades. The person experiencing the baptism and fulness of the Spirit has, it is claimed, a most wonderful life.

> 'It is a life of perfect rest. All unrest dishonours Christ. It is a life of perfect peace. To experience anything but peace – even under opposition, oppression, loss, bereavement, or perplexity – is to dishonour Christ and his Word. It is a life lived by the Christ dwelling in us, and therefore a life of perfect joy. Such a life is a victorious life – a life of constant miracle.'

Another bestseller, *The Holy Spirit and You*, by Dennis and Rita Bennett (founders, with others, of the charismatic movement in

America in the 1960s), includes health in the bliss of the Christian:–

> 'The Scriptures promise health for the believer . . . if we become ill, God will heal us. People say: "You're not going to live for ever. You've got to die sometime!" True. But long life is promised to God's people, and when we do go home to our Father, it is not necessary that we go in disease and pain.'

Suffering, to these teachers, is merely God's way of breaking down our reliance on self, and leading us to a total dependence upon him. Once this higher ground is attained, spiritual and physical trials and setbacks come to an end. Should any believer experience sadness, failure or loss of elevated feeling and assurance, it will be blamed on a failure of faith having allowed the flesh to reassert control.

These teachers unwittingly consign the apostles to the ranks of faithless, carnal Christians, not to mention the heroes of church history such as reformers and revival instruments. All these experienced tremendous suffering and constant setbacks, including frequent and serious health handicaps. Spirit-baptism teachers create images of spiritual experience which are unbiblical, unreal and highly emotional. They deny the Lord his right to draw the clouds across the heavens so that our warmer spiritual feelings are temporarily eclipsed. Scripture, however, teaches that these moments are the Lord's way of drawing out our deepest reserves of trust and love.

There are countless earnest believers who have been trained by Spirit-baptism teachers to equate spirituality with a kind of emotional 'high', or 'cloud nine' experience, and have been compelled to create within them a self-induced mood of religious excitement and joy. Such a rejection of suffering simply takes no account of the plain teaching of so much Scripture. Did not the Lord Jesus Christ, our perfect forerunner and example, experience suffering throughout his life? Was he not (even prior to Calvary) a 'man of sorrows, and acquainted with grief'? Yet our Saviour was the perfect man. He suffered reproach and heaviness but all without sin. It would be blasphemous to suggest that our Lord's life was anything but perfect and holy, or that his communion with the Father was ever clouded.

The apostles also knew great trials. Paul speaks of being troubled on every side, perplexed and persecuted. He tells us he was constantly delivered unto death for Jesus' sake. He speaks of having much tribulation, and no rest, with 'fightings without' and 'fears within'. He owns to being cast down and suffering the continual distress of a thorn in his flesh. He mentions infirmities, reproaches, necessities, persecutions, distresses and weakness. For his countrymen he had great heaviness and continual sorrow in his heart.* Was the apostle unspiritual in these feelings?

In that famous chapter, *Romans 8*, Paul says that we know that all things work together for our good, and that we may be more than conquerors, even though we feel the pain of suffering (v 18), and also of many other woes including nakedness, peril, sword and slaughter (vv 35-36). This is a deep subject which we cannot fully expound in this study, but true sanctification does not immunise us from troubles and distresses. Rather, it enables us to live through them upheld by the promise of *Isaiah 43.2* – 'When thou passest through the waters, I will be with thee; and through the rivers, they shall not overflow thee: when thou walkest through the fire, thou shalt not be burned; neither shall the flame kindle upon thee.'

There can be no credibility in any view of Spirit-baptism or of sanctification which takes no account of the place of suffering in the life of a believer. We cannot and must not respect a system which fails to acknowledge that part of our training in this life is to learn to trust the Lord in times of darkness and trial.

The same is true of bodily sickness. Although the apostle Paul could not heal Trophimus or Timothy (and gave the latter practical advice rather than healing), some Spirit-baptism writers insist that bodily sickness is not meant to persist in a believer. It is, they claim,

---

* See *2 Corinthians 4.8-9; 7.5; 12.7-10; Romans 9.1-3.*

either a punishment from God, or it is due to the believer's failure in seeking the fulness of the Spirit and the healing that this will bring. However, Scripture commends patient suffering in affliction and illness. While God may hear our prayers for healing, he may equally call us to prove him and witness to him in and through suffering.[*]

---

[*] See Dr Masters' book *The Healing Epidemic* (Wakeman Trust, London) for a full treatment of divine healing.

# 11
# The Case of the Ephesus Twelve

'And it came to pass, that, while Apollos was at Corinth, Paul having passed through the upper coasts came to Ephesus: and finding certain disciples, he said unto them, Have ye received the Holy Ghost since ye believed? And they said unto him, We have not so much as heard whether there be any Holy Ghost' *(Acts 19.1-2).*

WE HAVE OBSERVED that the *Acts* passage quoted here is a favourite proof text of those who teach the necessity of a baptism of the Spirit in addition to conversion (coupled with the gift of tongues). Does Paul's action of laying his hands on the 'Ephesus twelve' to impart the Holy Spirit justify these ideas? The answer is clearly and definitely not, for the following reasons.

The men Paul met were described by Luke as *disciples*, a term which he generally reserved for believers. It turned out that they had been baptised by disciples of John the Baptist, which tells us that they were undoubtedly Jews. (They were, by the way, not the same people who are mentioned in *Acts 18.26-27*, who were associated with Aquila and Priscilla at Ephesus. When Paul returned to the city he stumbled across this further group – the Ephesus twelve.)

The apostle wanted to know whether these men had experienced the Holy Spirit at the time they believed in Christ, but why was such a question in his mind? After all, Paul taught that *every* Christian receives the Spirit automatically at the time of conversion. (He states emphatically in *Romans 8.9* that if any man does not have the Spirit of Christ, he is not a true Christian.) Why, then, should Paul have thought it possible that the men had not received the Spirit when they believed in Christ? The explanation is that Paul suspected (rightly, as it turned out) that they had come to believe in Christ through the teaching of disciples of John the Baptist. In this case they would not have known a major part of the Gospel message, nor about the coming of the Holy Spirit at Pentecost.

John had taught that Jesus was the promised Messiah who would take away sin. He also preached the need for sincere repentance. John, however, died before the Lord went to Calvary, and many of his disciples migrated to various regions, teaching his incomplete message. Obviously this soon became out of date, because these migrant disciples knew little or nothing about Calvary, or the resurrection, or the coming of the Holy Spirit, or the founding of a separate New Testament church. Nor did they know that the Lord was now giving the New Testament Scriptures by revelation through apostles and prophets. People who heard the preaching of John's disciples received only a part of the Gospel message.

This was exactly the problem with Apollos *(Acts 18.24-26)*. Such people experienced genuine conviction of sin, repented before God, and put their trust in Christ as the One who would somehow take away the sin of the world, though they were not sure how. If they had heard of his crucifixion and resurrection, and embraced that, they probably knew nothing of the outpouring of the Spirit. They were born again, but much light was missing. Most of them were believers in a 'pre-Calvary' Messiah, and therefore stuck, so to speak, between the Testaments.

When Paul found the twelve disciples at Ephesus (perhaps holding their own prayer group in a corner of the synagogue) he recognised their sincerity and found that they relied upon Jesus as Messiah. But he was clearly puzzled by them. Where had they heard the Gospel? How had they been converted? Were they 'pre-Calvary' believers in the Messiah? Did they understand that the New Testament church was now distinct from the Temple and synagogues? Did they know about the new revelation being given through apostles authenticated by signs and wonders? Did they know about the coming of the Holy Spirit at Pentecost?

Paul's concern was to find out just what these men (who appeared to have no contact with other believers) knew about all these things. So he asked his question, which we expand for clarity, 'Did you have any knowledge or experience of the Holy Spirit when or since you heard and believed the message of Christ?' Their reply fully justified Paul's puzzlement over them. They looked at him in amazement and said, 'We have not so much as heard whether there be any Holy Ghost!'

This told Paul all he needed to know. He realised that although they were believers in Jesus as the Messiah, they had no idea that the promised Holy Spirit *had come*, and that the age of the New Testament church had started. He now knew that these pious souls had never come into contact with any mainstream Christian preachers, so he naturally asked them, 'Unto what then were ye baptised?' When they replied, 'Unto John's baptism', Paul's supposition about them was completely confirmed.

To take this passage, as second-blessing teachers do, and to regard these Ephesian disciples as if they were fully-fledged converts of Christian preachers, who needed a subsequent baptism of the Spirit, is a very odd and mistaken interpretation. As we have said, these men were caught in the gap between the Old and New Testaments.

While genuine believers, accepted by God, they did not enjoy full Gospel light. They probably knew little of Calvary, and nothing of Pentecost and the Holy Spirit until Paul explained all these things to them, then they were baptised in the name of the Lord Jesus. At the same time these unusual and atypical believers were granted a remarkable blessing, an outpouring of the Holy Spirit with the gifts of tongues and prophecy. In other words, they enjoyed a miniature reproduction of the Day of Pentecost.

Why should God have granted this unusual outpouring of spiritual gifts to these dozen men? Why would he grant a 'mini-Pentecost' some 23 years after that great event? The answer is that the Gospel was about to make great inroads into an entirely new and vast area. Each miniature Pentecost of the *Book of Acts* had the same important message. The outpouring upon the Samaritan converts (recorded in *Acts 8*) was significant because it communicated a vital message to Jewish Christians, who were commanded to accept Samaritan believers as true Christians, equal to themselves, and fully grafted into the church. And for their part the Samaritans (always frostily independent of Jerusalem) were shown that they should obey the apostles, and recognise one spiritual family, for there was now *one* church for all converts. (We note that there is no mention of tongues-speaking in Samaria, but the outpouring of the Spirit still ranks as a 'mini-Pentecost'.)

The outpouring of the Spirit at the house of Cornelius (recorded in *Acts 10*) again communicated this vital message to Jewish Christians, who were emphatically told by God that the Gentiles were accepted into the church.

The meeting of Paul with the twelve 'Johnites' at Ephesus counts as the third and final recorded 'mini-Pentecost', and like the other two it had the same overriding purpose, which is gleaned from what followed. We read in *Acts 19.8-10* of how Paul preached for two years in Ephesus, and how people throughout Asia heard the Word. There were very many Jews scattered in those parts, harbouring massive

Jewish prejudice against Gentiles and against the new church order. Even tender-hearted, believing Jews thought, 'Moses can never pass away! God has told us not to swerve in the slightest from the law of Moses! We must protect it and not let anyone add to it or take away from it. But this Christian church is all so new and so radical. These preachers are saying that our worship must change, and that the ceremonial is of no use. How can this be?'

It was in answer to such misgivings that the signs of Pentecost, designed to rebuke unbelieving Jews and to encourage all who gave up ceremonialism for Christ, were manifested in this vast, new region of outreach. Thus the Lord gave fresh tokens of Pentecost to twelve Jews of Ephesus to liberate their Jewish consciences and to authenticate his Truth. Perhaps no one in Ephesus beside these twelve men ever received the foreign-language gifts; there is no record that others did. In that region the healing gifts appear to have been given only to Paul *(Acts 19.11-12)*. Tongues are not mentioned in Paul's letter to the Ephesians written later, in about AD 60. Nevertheless, for the dozen or so men who formed the foundation of the new, regional church, God set his seal upon the authenticity of their church and mission in a remarkable way, and at the same time confirmed to other Jewish believers that they must move on with the church of Jesus Christ.

This leads us to the second idea which charismatic teachers derive from this event at Ephesus, namely, that in those days every believer who received the Spirit automatically spoke in tongues as evidence of having done so. This conclusion, however, does not tally with the record of *Acts* which shows that few people actually received the *outward* gifts and tokens of the Spirit when he was poured out. On the Day of Pentecost a maximum of 120 people spoke in tongues *(Acts 1.15* and *2.4)*. As we noted earlier, there is no mention of the 3,000 converts doing so, even though we are given considerable detail about the evidences of their new-found spiritual life. Possibly not *all* the 120 disciples spoke in tongues, for only the *men* seem to have been heard *(Acts 2.13)*. We must remember, also, that these tongues were real languages, understood by those who came from many different countries.

The vast number of additional people whose conversions are recorded in *Acts 4* did not speak in tongues. It is clear that as far as the biblical record is concerned, therefore, only a very small minority of people spoke in tongues around the time of Pentecost. (Statistically, the highest figure, if we adhere closely to the record, is below 2.5%.) In other words, while the promised gift of the Holy Spirit *himself* was given to every convert upon repentance *(Acts 2.38)*, yet the *outward sign-gifts* of the Spirit, which visibly authenticated his presence in the newly-formed church, were given only to a few select people, possibly all of these being men.

Furthermore, after the time of Pentecost there seems to have been a long period of silence as far as tongues-speaking is concerned. Signs and wonders certainly went on (as the Scripture says, by the hands of apostles) but tongues-speaking does not appear to have continued on a regular basis. The evidence for this is in *Acts* chapters 10 and 11, which describe events which took place at least six years after Pentecost. (This is the shortest estimate offered by conservative scholars. Some go as high as 13 years.) Tongues are seen again for the first time after all these years, and Peter appears to say that there had been no tongues-speaking during the intervening period. In *Acts 10* we are told about the wonderful conversion of Gentiles who gathered with Cornelius to listen to the preaching of Peter. As Peter was preaching, the Holy Spirit fell upon the gathered company, and they spoke in tongues, to the astonishment of the Jews who were with Peter. When Peter later recounted this to the gathered church members at Jerusalem, he expressed himself in a highly significant way, saying – 'And as I began to speak, the Holy Ghost fell on them, as on us *at the beginning*' *(Acts 11.15)*.

Peter did not say that the Holy Ghost gave tongues, just as he did every week in the church at Jerusalem. He referred everyone back to that remarkable phenomenon of Pentecost at least six years before. So unusual was this event, that it jarred Peter's mind to remember the words of Christ – 'John indeed baptised with water; but ye shall be baptised with the Holy Ghost.' He took these words as a reference to the general baptism of the Spirit poured out at Pentecost, and by quoting them he tells us how he viewed the event in the house of Cornelius. He saw it as a special event on a par with Pentecost, but obviously on a very much smaller scale. The message in this case was to the Jews, who needed to be convinced that believing Gentiles were fully-fledged members of the church of Jesus Christ.

The conversion of the Gentiles in the house of Cornelius took place between 6 and 13 years after Pentecost, and the Ephesus incident of tongues-speaking occurred 23 years after Pentecost – around AD 54. But there is no mention in the Scriptures of tongues-speaking taking place between the Cornelius incident and this occurrence at Ephesus, apart from the information we are given in *1 Corinthians 14.22* and *29*, where the apostle authorises a maximum of three people to contribute a message by tongues in a service as a sign-message to cynical Jews. From these few references to tongues we discover that they were a miraculous gift of foreign-language proph-ecies given by God to shock and convince Jews. This purpose prevails in all three of the 'mini-Pentecost' outpourings.

Clearly, then, every believer in New Testament times did not speak in tongues or prophesy. The miniature repetitions of Pente-cost, three in number (and only two including tongues-speaking), were each given for special reasons (and as a sign to Jews), and were never intended to be a picture of normal church life in the ongoing church age.

It is of very great importance that we realise that the teachings of Spirit-baptism groups including Pentecostalists and charismatics stand in complete opposition to 'traditional' evangelical doctrine. They are not merely slightly different, but are a point-by-point contradiction of the 'methods' of Scripture in matters of holiness, healing and assurance. When concerned believers really begin to study the texts, they invariably come to see how wide of the mark these ideas are, and how sure and glorious are the time-honoured doctrines of the Holy Spirit.

# The Charismatic Illusion
Co-author: John C. Whitcomb
*100 pages, paperback, ISBN 978 1 908919 70 0*

Now with more answers to questions asked by people investigating the arguments, this veteran book contends for the biblical position on the gifts that prevailed for nearly 2,000 years before the charismatic movement came along.

Here is the dynamic teaching of the Spirit that sustained true churches and believers through dark and bright years of history, through the Reformation, through the Puritan era, through the time of great Confessions of Faith, through repeated awakenings and revivals, and through the worldwide growth of the modern missionary movement.

Here is the case for authentic biblical spiritual life.

# The Healing Epidemic
*143 pages, paperback, ISBN 978 1 908919 24 3*

Dr Masters here answers the arguments used by healers in support of their methods. He explains Bible teaching on what demons can and cannot do, and how *James 5* should be implemented in churches today. He also proves that the conscious mind should always be switched on for spiritual activities. Included is a brilliant assessment of miraculous healing by a leading British medical professor.

'This volume is a masterful analysis and criticism of the most recent manifestations of charismatic phenomena...The exposition of *James 5.13-14* is excellent, and his analysis of the place of the mind in the Christian's experience is remarkable. The concluding chapter by a medical doctor is also insightful...This is one of the best books on this subject today. It should be widely read by concerned Christian people of all theological persuasions.'
– *Bibliotheca Sacra*

# The Personal Spiritual Life
*127 pages, paperback, ISBN 978 1 908919 20 5*

From the personal indwelling of the Holy Spirit to living a life of commitment these chapters stir and encourage readers to advance spiritually.

In what sense may we 'feel' the presence of the Lord? What was the apostle Paul's method for progress in holiness? How may we identify our spiritual gifts? And how may we count more for the Lord, and sustain spiritual joy?

These are among the themes of this tonic for present-day disciples of Christ.

# The Lord's Pattern for Prayer
*118 pages, paperback, ISBN 978 1 870855 36 5*

Subtitled – 'Studying the lessons and spiritual encouragements in the most famous of all prayers.' This volume is almost a manual on prayer, providing a real spur to the devotional life. The Lord's own plan and agenda for prayer – carefully amplified – takes us into the presence of the Father, to prove the privileges and power of God's promises to those who pray.

Chapters cover each petition in the Lord's Prayer. Here, too, are sections on remedies for problems in prayer, how to intercede for others, the reasons why God keeps us waiting for answers, and the nature of the prayer of faith.

# God's Rules for Holiness
## Unlocking the Ten Commandments
*139 pages, paperback, ISBN 978 1 870855 37 2*

Taken at face value the Ten Commandments are binding on all people, and will guard the way to Heaven, so that evil will never spoil its glory and purity. But the Commandments are far greater than their surface meaning, as this book shows.

They challenge us as Christians on a still wider range of sinful deeds and attitudes. They provide positive virtues as goals. And they give immense help for staying close to the Lord in our walk and worship.

The Commandments are vital for godly living and for greater blessing, but we need to enter into the panoramic view they provide for the standards and goals for redeemed people.

# Faith, Doubts, Trials and Assurance
*139 pages, paperback, ISBN 978 1 870855 50 1*

Ongoing faith is essential for answered prayer, effective service, spiritual stability and real communion with God. In this book many questions are answered about faith, such as – How may we assess the state of our faith? How can faith be strengthened? What are the most dangerous doubts? How should difficult doubts be handled? What is the biblical attitude to trials? How can we tell if troubles are intended to chastise or to refine? What can be done to obtain assurance? What are the sources of assurance? Can a believer commit the unpardonable sin? Exactly how is the Lord's presence felt?

Dr Masters provides answers, with much pastoral advice, drawing on Scripture throughout.

# Steps for Guidance
## In the Journey of Life
*134 pages, paperback, ISBN 978 1 870855 66 2*

In recent years the subject of how to find God's guidance has become controversial. Some say that God does not have a specific plan for the lives of his people, but allows us to please ourselves. Others say God's will is known by dreams, visions, and 'words of knowledge'.

By contrast with these sadly unbiblical ideas, this book presents the time-honoured, scriptural view that Christians must seek God's will in all the major decisions of life, such as career, marriage, location, and church. Six essential steps are traced from the Bible, and principles are given on additional practical issues such as possessions and leisure activities; ambition and wealth; joining or leaving a church.

Here is a strong challenge to authentic Christian commitment, with an abundance of pastoral advice.

# Church Membership in the Bible
*61 pages, paperback, ISBN 978 1 870855 64 8*

Christ has designed a 'home' or family for his people, described in these pages as an accomplishment of divine genius. This is a magnificent subject, vital to spiritual growth and blessing and also to our service for the Saviour.

This book answers many questions about churches and church membership in New Testament times. Next to having a real walk with Christ and knowing the doctrines of the faith, membership of a good church has a powerful formative influence on the believer's life.

# The Faith
## Great Christian Truths
*119 pages, paperback, ISBN 978 1 870855 54 9*

There is nothing like this popular, non-technical sweep through key themes of the Christian faith, highlighting very many inspiring and enlivening points. It often takes an unusual approach to a topic in order to bring out the full wonder and significance. It is designed to be enjoyed by seasoned Christians, and also by all who want to explore the great features of the faith, and discover the life of the soul.

CONTENTS:

| | |
|---|---|
| The Mysterious Nature of a Soul | The New Birth |
| What God is Actually Like | Why the Resurrection? |
| The Fall of Man | Prophecies of Resurrection |
| The Three Dark Hours of Calvary | The Holy Trinity |

# Worship in the Melting Pot
*148 pages, paperback, ISBN 978 1 870855 33 4*

'Worship is truly in the melting pot,' says the author. 'A new style of praise has swept into evangelical life shaking to the foundations traditional concepts and attitudes.' How should we react? Is it all just a matter of taste and age? Will churches be helped, or changed beyond recognition?

This book presents four essential principles which Jesus Christ laid down for worship, and by which every new idea must be judged.

Here also is a fascinating view of how they worshipped in Bible times, including their rules for the use of instruments, and the question is answered – What does the Bible teach about the content and order of a service of worship today?

# Not Like Any Other Book
## Interpreting the Bible
*161 pages, paperback, ISBN 978 1 870855 43 3*

Faulty Bible interpretation lies at the root of every major mistake and 'ism' assailing churches today, and countless Christians are asking for the old, traditional and proven way of handling the Bible to be spelled out plainly.

A new approach to interpretation has also gripped many evangelical seminaries and Bible colleges, an approach based on the ideas of unbelieving critics, stripping the Bible of God's message, and leaving pastors impoverished in their preaching.

This book reveals what is happening, providing many brief examples of right and wrong interpretation. The author shows that the Bible includes its own rules of interpretation, and every believer should know what these are.

# Do We Have a Policy?
## Paul's Ten Point Policy for Church Health & Growth
*93 pages, paperback, ISBN 978 1 870855 30 3*

What are our aims for the shaping of our church fellowship, and for its growth? Do we have an agenda or framework of desired objectives? The apostle Paul had a very definite policy, and called it his 'purpose', using a Greek word which means – a plan or strategy displayed for all to see.

This book sets out ten policy ideals, gleaned from Paul's teaching, all of which are essential for the health and growth of a congregation today.

For a full listing of Wakeman titles please see www.wakemantrust.org